Barbara Hanrahan was born in Adelaide in 1939, and studied art in Australia and then England, where her first three books, *The Scent of Eucalyptus* (1973), *Sea-Green* (1974) and *The Albatross Muff* (1977) appeared.

Well known as an artist as well as an author, her work is displayed in the National Gallery of Australia and in most other State galleries, and she has exhibited in Australia, Britain, Japan and Italy.

Barbara Hanrahan's books include *Where the Queens All Strayed* (1979), *The Peach Groves* (1980), *The Frangipani Gardens* (1981), *Dove* (1983), *Kewpie Doll* (1984, the sequel to *The Scent of Eucalyptus*), *Annie Magdalene* (1985), *Dream People* (1987) and *A Chelsea Girl* (1988). She now lives in Adelaide.

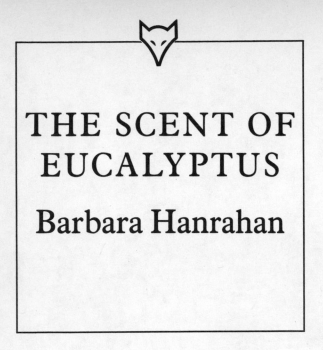

THE SCENT OF EUCALYPTUS

Barbara Hanrahan

THE HOGARTH PRESS

LONDON

Published in 1989 by
The Hogarth Press
30 Bedford Square
London WC1B 3SG

First published in Great Britain by Chatto & Windus, 1973

A CIP catalogue record for this book is available from the British Library.

ISBN 0 7012 0855 4

Printed in Finland by
Werner Söderström Oy

See with what simplicity
This Nymph begins her golden days!
In the green Grass she loves to lie,
And there with her fair Aspect tames
The Wilder flow'rs, and gives them names:
But only with the Roses plays;
    And them does tell
What Colour best becomes them, and what Smell.

ANDREW MARVELL

ONE

My mother hedged about my birth: said she found me in a rose. And I believed her—saw myself pink and perfect as a rubber dolly, added some modest gauze, even a little crown. Of course I went too far—tried to make it perfect; cheated with shears and a crisscross net—no thorns or suckers, gall or fly or chafer.

My mother lied—that rose-birth wasn't true. I was born the same as any other. Stripped of any past pretensions to wisdom, I entered the world; lay naked before strangers who meant nothing to me, but to whom I, by my very helplessness, meant a lot.

I was offered as a sop to strangers—a sop for hoarded (but unacknowledged) disappointments. I was a prize, presented on an off-chance, that for an instant deceived—tricked them into thinking that real life bore some resemblance to the thing they thought was life: a wan pretence fabricated by newspapers and politicians; made safe by shops that sold lounge suites and latest season's costumes on hire-purchase, bearable by wireless jingles and long-range forecasts.

That paltry thing they were offered bound insidiously—in a moment that became all future time. It fastened closely—yet never completely. It erased with cheap comforts the original world—yet never entirely. In the end it dissolved—but always too late. They were left free when there was nothing to be free for; bled so empty there was nothing left them, but to dissolve as well.

I was born in Adelaide in September, with a birthmark on my neck and an excitement mark on my left cheek. The birthmark was arrested, and faded to a pale snarl. The excitement mark was more wily, escaped detection, and was left to flicker on and off—a perpetual warning of something yet to come.

I had a father, but he died. Three months after that I was in a hospital too. I tricked them—lived; came home to five.

Three of them were important—graved themselves for ever. Two became objects on a mantelpiece.

My great-grandfather left a bell that he rang in a last illness—a bell of brass rimmed with fruit like apples, and leaves the poet called acanthus. He left a purse that opened to reveal empty pockets and a silver clasp, a compass with a querulous face, a china inkwell painted with a China-rose, a penknife. And a photograph of himself sitting in the sun, and a name—I called him Little White Puppy, because of his hair—because I couldn't say 'Papa'.

My great-grandmother betrayed herself with less: a bleached cameo carved with someone who could have been her, a tray-cloth sprigged with iron-mould and satin-stitch poppies, a photograph of herself with spectacles, stockings in folds, slippers with pompons.

(How is it that the bell, the purse, the compass, the inkwell, the knife and cameo and tray-cloth should live on? Why is it that their owners should be preserved so perfect in their endings on the green album page—like

8

odourless flowers from an ancient wedding, a dead favourite's curl, butterflies behind glass, silver-paper pictures: he, in the sun; she, in blank spectacles before sweet peas? And how did a baker become just a bell? Why the spinster an iron-mould speck? Once he was twenty-seven and had a name—George Henry Nobes, and he married her, and she was Elizabeth Davis—his Stella, his Beatrice, his Lesbia. And she was twenty-one, and it was 1889.)

My great-grandfather was born in Cornwall—came to Australia as a boy in one of the last sailing-ships; as an old man signed his name in the register under the gum-tree at Glenelg. My great-grandfather was a baker who was too generous: gave countless Depression loaves on credit, went into liquidation. Always helpful, he ushered in his end: held the gate for them when they came to put out the fire in the shed—the ladder hit him on the head, and he died at eighty-four.

My great-grandmother, that Stella of the speckled mould, was born at Houghton in the Adelaide Hills. Her father was an adventurer who died seeking El Dorado at Alice Springs. Her mother was Welsh. She had three sisters and a brother: Poll and Mill and Annie and Jack. Some of them were people I knew.

There was a sepia picture of Poll with an ostrich feather bonnet and a studio palm-tree. I remembered her in a simpler setting—visiting us from the hills, a shrunken lady, her sisters dead, bringing country eggs and honey with a comb. I walked down the path with her and she pulled up my sock by the agapanthus—and there was lovely warmth I didn't know was sensual, and I felt dizzy.

THE SCENT OF EUCALYPTUS

Poll married Will from the jam factory. They lived at Houghton in a house with a balcony and the scent of eucalyptus all about. I saw a spaniel and a lavatory starred with ash and a centipede surprised me from a tree. I saw Jack, who was a bachelor I had to kiss, and a little strange, but harmless—just toy tanks in a bedroom. Mill was a brittle ghost who got engaged but broke it off and straddled a Colombo rickshaw. Annie was but a name. Elizabeth was my great-grandmother.

She went, vanished utterly—leaving behind four children that do not exist.

Once I clasped the creased fingers of one of them and walked to a cemetery. We crossed a railway line and tramped on parklands between cows. Murmuring voices, flickers of pink from the willows meant lovers were about.

I wanted to stop, but she pulled me on to a strange landscape where Jesus and all His angels and the Lamb of God faced convolvulus and waist-high grass. The fight was almost over—but the lovely angel smiled, flourished her Turk's-cap lily. And there were rusting tin leaves and china garlands and glassy domes.

When we reached the baker and his Stella, they were further from us than ever. There were no eyes to see, no ears to hear, not even a mouth—just silence, and the child who was my grandmother looked sad. We turned away (she couldn't look sad for ever), and marched on past the dead tended with watering-cans and lonely fingers. And there was another plot and other sterile hopes and expectations. But it hurt more this time, for it was my father. And we celebrated him with loosepetalled roses. And the poet that lived on dangerously said things about heedless marble.

I stood before the slab that bore his name—and it was my name. I gazed at the letters and they were grimed with dirt (the railway was very near). The willows were too—and was he ever a lover, ever my father? But I swept away abstraction—made it bearable and related him to me. For by being my father he lived a life—didn't he? He did that anyway—didn't he? But died.

And the uneasy poet quoted raindrops and milky skies —for it was September then, when I was born. An Australian September—therefore the spring. And the poet let him have it too. For the rains and skies were there for him as well—one year later at his death.

TWO

As a child and ever after, the minute, hidden facets of things intrigued me. I was for ever walking with my head bent, looking at the ground. I saw an ant picking its way across the earth, the moss at the base of the wall, the wings of the bee in the hyssop. I watched the shadow-play the rose leaves made on the fence. I saw the ant run under a leaf, over a stone, past seed-pods into a hole. I peered into the clipped stems of the valerian and saw greenness. I saw bulbs slit by greener spears. I saw the red geranium turn black and clenched dots turned mauve and into lilacs. And the ant came out of its hole, clambered over a pebble, a needle of grass — was lost amongst the ivy.

I came inside, and found the dust that lay under the mat, the stale hair in the brush, the soap's awful underside like a sweating sore. I watched a shadow garden of pot-plants bloom on the wall, the bubbles that danced in the saucepan. I saw the pleated linings of mushrooms, tomatoes ruffled by stars, carrots hung with tassels. I forgot the mould that flecked the lemon, maggots in the bin, dead flowers that smelt of ponds.

I came closer to the three who were important: to the grandmother, and saw the hair in her nostril, the dirt between her toes, dye spots in her scalp; to the great-aunt, and her parting was thick with scurf, she had wax-buds in her ear, a sour handkerchief up her sleeve. And my mother tried not to cry: face all crumpled, eyes gone blurry, ugly mouth square. I watched unmoved.

My grandmother was rooted in her garden, with cheeks ripped by thorns, mud-bruised legs, skirts always caught on a brier. The great-aunt reigned in the house: she flapped her arms and bread-crumbs and the table-cloth cut the air; she hurled knives and the apostle spoons to a silver streak. The mother tended us all: with snail-curls and lavender setting-lotion, and a needle fly-ing on over endless wefts and warps — on and on.

My mother was elusive. I did not possess her. The grandmother and great-aunt were always there, but when I awoke she was gone: came home with the street lights, and then I didn't know her. I met a stranger at the tram stop, and I couldn't kiss her cheek. She wasn't the same. Not my mother: smiling through a veil of spots and smelling like violets, with hair made Hot Chestnut, and eyes gone little with black, and a coral smile. Her heels were high, her leather toes so pointed, and she pounced in a fox-trimmed coat. (I wanted her as the other, when I felt her up against me in the bed and saw her face all small without the make-up, and shiny from dry-skin cream. And I saw the dots she let me squeeze beside her mouth, and knew the mole was there upon her back, but hidden by the nightie. She almost had no breasts, they were so small, and she was ashamed, and when the other person went out they were stuffed with handkerchiefs — I watched her put them in. Her hair was so fine she put it up every night, and under the net were rows of bobby-pin curls. I could even see a bit of

13

pale scalp, and that made it better—she was even more mine. She was gentle like a Chinese or a quiet mouse.) When she put on the Hot Chestnut and the waves and the tortoise-shell combs and the side-bow when it came in fashion, it was different. She was almost like a princess —someone else's mother, and I did not know her then.

For reasons I could not comprehend the princess slept beside me in the brass bed and led me to the lavatory at night. She was my mother. I linked her with the Little Mermaid and the Snow Queen. Strange ladies in trams compared her to Vivien Leigh in *Gone with the Wind*, or said the pair of us resembled the Duchess of Kent and dear little Princess Alex.

My mother was complicated. She had personalities nesting one inside the other like Chinese boxes. She hid her innate romanticism and its attendant vices—timidity, tremulousness, sensitivity—under the swathes of her veil; stamped them with her heels, smothered them in her fox-trimmed coat. But still they flourished—sliced her onion disguise.

At fourteen she put away the navy tunic, the blazer, the striped tie and left the school where she learned to say '*Bonjour, monsieur*,' and '*Comprenez-vous français?*' and wrote the prize-winning essay bound in grosgrain ribbon. It was the Depression, and she began work at a hairdresser's in the Arcade, answering the telephone for two shillings and sixpence. A few weeks later she showed the Staff Manager at one of the big Rundle Street stores the drawings she had made. She became an artist.

By day she drew cork-soled sandals, tiger-striped lounge suites, wirelesses like Aztec temples. At night she became Rambling Rose and competed with the

Tommy Tadpoles, Broom Witches, Star Maidens, and Happy Jacks of Adelaide for lilac, blue, and pink certificates for stories and poems and drawings in the *Sunday Mail*'s Children's Page.

She grew older. She sewed puff-sleeved peasant blouses, monogrammed chiffon and feather-bordered scarves. She had a favourite evening frock with a fish-tail train and décolleté back. Her hem was weighed down with pennies; she tucked handkerchiefs inside her front. She read Ella Wheeler Wilcox, collected for her Glory Box, bought coffee-coloured underwear, pinned a gardenia to her wrist at tea-dances.

She met my father at a dance in the King's Ballroom. His name was Maurice, but they called him Bob. He looked like Tyrone Power. He looked charming, and he was — 'But moody,' they said. Different from the others, he was a gentleman — pronounced cock: 'coh'. He read a newspaper in a corner all night; watched her; took her home.

They were married at Holy Trinity on North Terrace, just past the railway bridge.

For a while they lived with Grandfather Hanrahan in Dew Street. But he got drunk; accused my mother of steaming his letters. He locked the letter-box and my mother pried with a pin: broke it. There was a row and they left.

My mother longed for security. My father strained from the tameness of marriage — from the sameness and mediocrity of the machine-shop at Holdens.

While she was giving birth to me at St. Ives, he found the thirty pounds she had hidden in the wardrobe to pay the bill: took it, and bought drinks for Jock Beresford and Fred Juncken and all the others whose names are forgotten. He got drunk and wrecked a billiard saloon; she had to pay for the damage and see the Sergeant at the Thebarton Police Station. He carried me into the bar of the Hotel Gambier in Light Square, and she found us there — him: the bookmaker, with her navy bag round his neck, taking bets on me: the prize. He told my grandmother at her own front door that she was no plum. 'It all comes from marrying a Catholic,' they said.

One evening in winter, riding his bicycle to work for the night-shift, my father got wet in the rain. He caught cold; refused to take care of himself. The cold got worse — went from influenza to pneumonia to tuberculosis. He was taken to the Adelaide Hospital. He seemed to get better — asked for a newspaper to read the race results. The next day he was dead. My mother remembered his face.

My father died on the seventh of September, 1940 — the day after my first birthday. He was twenty-six.

My mother had a nervous breakdown. She sat in the sun in a canework armchair; her feet on the red-brick path, her eyes raw from crying. Three months later I ate an ice-block and she woke to find my body burning, my feet cold. I was taken to a hospital, like my father before me. They thought I would die.

My mother and grandmother came to watch me through the glass. I was better. I sat up and there was a pink hand and bananas and jelly in a little dish. The hand came closer and then it went away. It went to the next bed — I cried, and my mother cried too.

She went back to work. She went each day in a tram and a creaking lift to an office on a fourth floor. She sat there, from nine to five (with an hour off for lunch). And there were waxen dummies like pretty ladies and bias-cut dresses and satin underwear and other dresses that were patriotic in red and white and blue. She forgot herself at a drawing-board; dedicated herself to cigarette cases, vases, snoods, mirrors with sunrays, compacts with flying-fish.

Death only happened in newspapers. And it was nice to read of other people's husbands killed for ever in a war so far away. Death was clever, but she knew tricks. And beat him with price tags that said *take me* and wicked tilted hats. And with gossip in the lav with Norma and frog-cakes at lunch with Melveen. And there was Frank the office boy, and Janet the typist, and Des the copy-writer, and Wilf—only he died.

My mother was a lark whose tongue was cut; a gull with clipped wings. She learnt to expect nothing that she did not strive for. (She keeps her eyes to the ground and sees the dog shit and the old men's phlegm—that way she doesn't trip).

Gardenia wrists and coffee-coloured underwear, Glory Box and Ella Wheeler Wilcox disappeared. Their places were taken by chocolates in bed and a single cigarette, by *Vogue* and *Vanity Fair*, by Madame Weigel patterns; by things the same, but different.

The same, in that they were fanciful means of escape; different, in that unlike gardenia and Ella Wheeler they led precisely nowhere—promised nothing.

(The fancies turn into fetishes, and she doesn't even know it. Just washes the gloves and pats them dry with love. Does her nails and rinses out the stockings, curls

17

her hair and wishes the lines away. The names of Rubin-
stein and Arden are honoured in our house; little satin
labels stud her clothes. Cold cream is rubbed in slavishly,
elbows raped with pumice. She puts up her hair in a
Victory Roll.)

My mother trod a familiar path; hedged by as many
briers as Sleeping Beauty's ever was. (For briers that
are invisible pluck just as surely, just as bloody as any
others.) Her path led from a gate that shut with a click,
down grey ribbons of asphalt to a tram stop. She went
each day in a tram and a creaking lift to an office on a
fourth floor; sat there, from nine to five (with an hour off
for lunch). And when the bell rang, and she came out
with all the others—Norma and Melveen, Frank and
Janet and Des—her parcels were stuck with tickets to
show they were not stolen. Under her gloves her fingers
were stained with ink and Poster Black; but she didn't
care—it came off with scented soap at home.

So the days pass and the years tick away on the watch
that doesn't always go.

THREE

My GREAT-GRANDMOTHER gave birth to four children: two boys and two girls.

The boys grew from solemn, sepia, photograph figures in sailor suits to men.

The older, with his bird-like face and tawny fringe of hair, who held a cricket bat carelessly in his hand, was elected to take part in a stronger tragedy than most. He married a girl with black hair and blue eyes who spent her childhood in an orphanage because her mother and father were not married. Years later she found out who they were—but it was awkward: they had a respectable position, quite flash, and five other children, and she was a little common (it was the orphanage). So they didn't see her quite so often—after all, it wasn't as if they really knew her, and then she didn't come at all. And silly girl—not pretty any more—she drank herself to death. Willie, too, acted out his part faithfully. He, who was his mother's darling, disintegrated into a wrinkled wild-eyed ruin—a wine-dot, a dirty alcoholic—who died, with abundance all about him, of malnutrition in a tin shed.

The younger, propped up by a telescopic stick on a padded armchair, abandoned his toy whip, his pleated skirts and sailor's cap for a khaki uniform. He, with his smooth face and prim mouth married, because he must, Fanny, the publican's daughter. They had eleven children. Fanny's ginger hair and garrulous voice faded with time and cancer; she lay still at last, withered and drained of all her passion: her face as yellow as her faded hair against hospital sheets. Dick, of the smooth peach-bloom and wide-brimmed slouch hat became a stout, bald-headed worthy, who died, speechless from a brain haemorrhage, alone in a lavatory. He left a respectable Catholic aura and eight of the eleven children and twenty-three grandchildren behind him.

The girls were separated from each other by twenty years. One was my grandmother, the other my great-aunt.

Reece is my great-aunt; yet at ten I am taller than she at thirty-five. She is my grandmother's sister; yet she cannot read or write or count. She is a grown-up; yet she wears children's clothing. She has frog-like eyes with half-moon lids, sad eyebrows arched in permanent surprise, a domed forehead with wrinkles, a snout, a mouth that shows her tongue — becomes an idiot-grin when she is happy. People stare at her in the street — she is real, and reality is too strong for their slumbering, narcotized lives. She is a mongol.

That was what the book with the pictures of pop-eyes, hunch-backs, Siamese-twins, swollen-heads, web-fingers, lock-jaws, wry-necks said. The cover had a stain on it like snail slime. It made me feel sick, like the mad king's signature in the *Girl's Own Annual* of 1911.

(But the medical book lied — it was evil. It made me feel ashamed of Reece. It made me see her as a case-history, a circus freak; something to be petted, pitied, locked away for ever.)

THE SCENT OF EUCALYPTUS

The mongol is my great-aunt, who has been given three Christian names: Laurel Gwenda Reece — and is proud of them. She boasts of a boy friend called Reggie Aire. She sings 'K-K-K-Katy' and 'Daisy, Daisy' for me. She keeps her Christmas powders and perfumes and soaps in the drawer with her handkerchiefs; when she has a cold she smells of talcum powder, lily-of-the-valley, ashes of roses. She changes her dress in the afternoon; comes back from the bedroom with smudges of Pond's Peach Powder on her cheeks, mouth touched discreetly with red, lavender-water behind her ears. She begs pardon politely when she farts and looks ashamed.

My great-aunt is a martinet whom I must obey. She flourishes her broom like some Old Testament prophet, crying 'Cease!' or 'Holy Moses!' when I talk too much. She spends her days at special tasks, carried out in a rigid, unchanging order. She sweeps the kitchen, polishes the floor, cleans the bath with Gumption, sets the table, shakes the tea-leaves onto the geraniums showing her garters, boils the handkerchiefs in salt, does the ironing.

She likes ironing. She unpegs the dry washing, collects it in the wicker basket; sprinkles a benediction over handkerchiefs, table-cloths, bloomers, petticoats, night-dresses — reduces them to the same tight sausage bundles. Her spit sizzles on the iron as she tests its heat. She toils happily, elbow sticking out, red in the face; turning the handkerchiefs into triangles, quartering the table-cloths, folding the bloomers to sexless halves; nosing her iron through petticoat shallows of pin-tucks and pleats, guiding it to safe harbour through virginal excesses of night-dress folds.

Reece wears lisle stockings she darns on a wooden mushroom, pleated skirts that stick out behind, aprons that bloom with flowers, faded winceyette nighties, a brassière Nan takes tucks in, felt slippers, patent leather shoes, a shell-stitch cocoon of cardigans. She dresses in bed on winter mornings: sits cross-legged between the sheets—an aged kewpie doll, skirts spread fanwise, mustering courage to climb into fleecy knickers.

She is at her ease in these familiar, slightly grubby garments—she looks ridiculous on special occasions, costumed in her best. Then, with her body strangely stiff, her face naked from the removal of the hair along her lip, ringlets round her brow, mouth prissily pursed, trying to look alert but succeeding only in looking stupid, she is Nan's despair.

Reece had a succession of celluloid dolls called always Peggy. She had as well a sewing-box, a paint-box, families of coloured pencils in plastic envelopes, a pencil-sharpener shaped like the world, a budgerigar called Tony.

Reece knitted face flannels in sugar-pink and pale pea-green, crooked squares Nan sewed to patchwork quilts, bed-socks of red and yellow that tied with satin bows. Her knitting was always in plain stitch—purl was too hard; Nan always cast on and off—she did it too loose. She sat with the crinkly balls tangling in her lap, one leg tucked under, only stopping when it was time to make the tea.

Reece was a stoic: she did not flinch when the bright rose of St. Anthony's fire blossomed on her face and they pulled her eye-lashes out and sheets dripping disinfectant were hung about the house.

Sometimes Reece was sick. Then, her needles silent, her hands empty, she lay in bed: her face all ashy, her cheeks gone sunken, the circles beneath her eyes swollen to ugly bladders. One day I watched her retching into the pot: shoulders shaking, brown eyes filled with tears. And I saw her in the bath: so skinny—her bones showing through sallow flesh, and withered breasts with bruised plum nipples, a beard between her legs.

When I was lazy I ordered Reece to fetch things for me, told her she was my slant-eyed Japanese servant. When I was ill she brought me food on a tray, wiped the sweat with a flannel. I liked her to wash my arms and legs with her soft clumsy hands; dry them with pats through the towel.

I thanked her then, but sometimes I was cruel.

There were days when I taunted her, confused her with questions; scolded her when she slept in her singlet and sat on one leg—told her she was dirty, told her she would stop the blood. There were days when I discovered the pot of urine in the wardrobe and ran to tell my mother; days when I reminded her of the rattle in her belly, the smacking sound her mouth made when she ate.

She stumbled blindly away, denying she was crying—locked herself in the bathroom.

And I was pierced with lovely, painful joy.

I crept after her; stooped at the keyhole; examined her shamelessly, like a specimen under glass. I watched, as she fumblingly took off her glasses; watched, as red-eyed and gulping, she washed her poor, crumpled face.

And she came out trembling, white-faced under a layer of powder, falsely smiling.

And I turned coward and tried to comfort her and soothe her — scared that Nan might find me out.

Reece remembered her mother. She watched my reaction slyly, as she told me she was in Heaven with the Angels, dropping her voice to the reverential, pious moo she thought she should.

But my great-grandmother, who gave birth gladly to Willie and Dick and Iris, was horrified at Reece's birth. It was Iris, twenty years older, who looked after her. For a while they were separated by marriage — with widowhood they came together. The relationship that both frustrated and fulfilled my grandmother's life began.

My grandmother ministers her life away in service to an eternal child.

She pares the child's corns, searches for wax in her ears, attacks her moustache with tweezers, curls her hair with spit and bobby-pins, cuts her nails when they are soft after the bath, rubs balm on her chilblains, inserts pessaries for constipation.

Nan and Reece share each other's bath water, sleep in twin beds.

When they are both old they huddle together in the room that is so cold and smells of silence. They are strangely altered: Reece, become even smaller; Iris, changed for ever from the ruddy Jewess in crêpe-marocain, smiling at her future in the sepia photograph — not even any more the grandmother I knew, but a wrinkled lady who cries in secret. They sit together before the slit eye of the electric fire; before the changing images that never change on the flickering television. Sometimes they link hands over the leaves that swirl statically on the carpet. Sometimes Reece's fingers caress her sister's cheek.

They are a pair.

FOUR

IRIS PEARL was the baker's daughter.

She drove a little trap; rode the cart-horse on the sand at Largs Bay (he kicked her head, and I felt the hollow—still there, after all those years). She ran the sewing-machine through her finger; had pleurisy (slept in a tent, blew into bottles, mustard-ointment rubbed on her chest); was stranded in a boat with Alec Luckett (his was the book-mark with the shadow-letter IRIS). She collected peacock-feathers; made silver-paper pictures, shell boxes, a table-runner with carnations; played the piano from sixpenny populars of 'Teasing' and 'Hearts and Flowers' and 'Fairy Wedding Waltz'.

Her tea-set was painted with ox-eye daisies. She sewed pockets for a night-dress and serviettes—trimmed them with crochet, Roman cut-work, Maltese edging.

She pinned a cameo of ivory to a collar that was high, put bandeaux of rose-buds in her hair. She had jabots of lawn and Valenciennes insertions; long-sleeved chemisettes with soutache braid on Brussels net. She had a hat of écru muslin, a petticoat of nainsook, a cover for a corset sprigged with shamrocks. She did her hair in plaited ear-phones; in the fashionable Récamier; like Psyche with glacé silk.

Iris Pearl was the baker's daughter.

She met the policeman from Terowie on the beach. Her necklace broke, and he was there to catch the pearls — to ask her out. They married at a Methodist manse in June (before the roses). When he died, four years later, the Police Band played at the funeral. The next year she put a poem in the *Advertiser*:

> *We who loved you sadly miss you*
> *As there dawns another year,*
> *And in lonely hours of thinking,*
> *Thoughts of you are ever dear.*

Charles Ebenezer, son of Jessie, died at thirty, when my mother was two years old. He was allowed up too soon after a routine operation for appendicitis, and died from a clot of blood on the day he was to come home.

My grandfather, younger then than I am now: a romantic, who wore a heart of New Zealand greenstone on his watch-chain; a chameleon, who hid behind a uniform, blew a silver whistle.

He had a Bible with pictures at the back: smudged pink and buff views of the Brook Kedron, the Mosque of Omar, the Wailing Wall. There were plump Dianas with lemon-drop breasts, Chaldean temples, Sennacherib's prism, the sun-god (Shamash) in his shrine — but only black and white.

He painted drummer-boys framed by garlands of roses; read Byron, Longfellow, Mrs. Hemans bound in calf. He printed EX LIBRIS: C. E. GOODRIDGE on each fly-leaf, drew a profile that brooded by 'On Leaving Newstead Abbey', penned on Mrs. Hemans in Gothic that was wobbly:

THE SCENT OF EUCALYPTUS

From
MOTHER
MAY XIX MDCCCCXIII
*Being the 24th. Anniversary
of my*
BIRTHDAY

Adam Lindsay Gordon, who had been in the South Australian Police Force too, was important to him, and on the first page of his *Collected Poems* he wrote:

> *May the Devil with a fiendish yell,*
> *With toasting fork and sulphur smell,*
> *Burn the churl in hottest Hell,*
> *Neglecting to return this book TO:*

followed by his signature, underneath.

After his death Iris went back to the bakery; became the dutiful daughter, served in the shop, looked after Reece. Perhaps she still dreamed; read novels called *The Scarlet Kiss, Pink Purity, The Wild Widow*; played her piano *diminuendo* in the dusk; sighed over Valentino; waited for her Sheik.

He came.

She married the station-master at Outer Harbour.

(Other than his name, Hugh, there was little more I knew, for my grandmother and mother refused to talk of him. He buried for ever Iris, the lusty girl. He cast a pall over the childhood of my mother. He was perverted, sadistic, cruel.

28

'What did he do?' I asked.

But it was hopeless: they said that some things were best not talked of—it doesn't do any good, you know, to bring it up again—least said, soonest forgotten. And besides, it still hurt. My mother, when pressed, brought herself to tell that he drowned puppies and kittens and made her watch; that he trod on her fingers when she played at his feet. Then her voice trailed off; she refused to probe deeper. I did not ask again.)

The station-master ran from marriage to Murray Bridge, taking a young girl with him—pursued by Iris, her sister-in-law, the young girl's parents.

With the divorce, the fiasco of my grandmother's second marriage was forgotten. Charles Ebenezer's picture hung in the dining-room at Rose Street with the coloured reproduction of the Bluff at Victor Harbour and the dear little thumb-in-mouth girl, lost for ever on the sands of Dee. I stared at him high above the sideboard. I could not link his silver-buttoned perfection with the Iris I knew.

Gone, were the nainsook petticoats and the rose-bud bandeaux. Gone, was the Iris who rode the horse on the sand, who painted ox-eyes on the tea-cup, and combined weaving-stitch and crochet with the point de Venise.

In her place was the Iris who sprinkled tea-leaves in the ashes when she cleaned the grate, who rolled pastry with a bottle, who remembered to heat the knitting-needle before she tested the cake, who banished iron-mould from the tablecloth with lemon juice and salt.

This Iris was my grandmother. She ruled the house,

shielded from the fickle arrows of fortune by a potent armoury of remedies.

She told me: 'To revive a sick aspidistra, push a rusty nail into the soil and keep it well watered. A discoloured neck will become as white as snow with a bleach of equal parts of glycerine and lemon juice applied before retiring. A few drops of castor oil on the roots of ferns will produce an abundance of new shoots. Cold tea-leaves bound on a burn take the pain away at once. A small piece of orris-root placed in the copper will impart a lasting fragrance to handkerchiefs and lingerie.'

Charles Ebenezer's wedding-ring still bit her finger next to the diamond, and she even had a marcasite eternity-ring she bought herself. But her fingers were red and slippery, and had broken nails and sometimes a plaster. They went puffy in winter with chilblains and when she did the washing they were pleated like the end of the copper-stick, stained from the blue-bag. And I watched her all humped with her stomach sticking out as she rubbed at the wash-board with Velvet soap, and thought how funny it was that she should ever have been another.

(I was deceived by familiarity. I didn't see, couldn't hear, forgot to reason.)

Inside the workaday Iris of the ruined hands, the young girl lived on; protected by the blur of memory, chaperoned by the constant shadow, Reece. She was there for me to see in the innocent blue eyes (I didn't see); there for me to hear in the hesitating, childlike voice that surprised me on the telephone (I didn't hear). She was there in the terrible depressions, smothering possessiveness, crippling self-pity that baffled me. She accounted for the copies of *True Romance*, *True Story*, *True Confessions* that were hidden beneath the mattress as surely as she did for my grandmother's shyness that isolated her, made her lonely.

And I knew her not. I only saw the Iris whose shoulders drooped from the shopping bags; who looked after Reece for forty years; who was my grandmother.

Iris is my grandmother. She has forget-me-not eyes, bushy eyebrows, rosy cheeks, silver hair she hides behind a rinse. Her face burns to brick in summer, but her body under the dresses that are always wash-day damp is white.

I know, for I slip into the bathroom when she forgets to lock the door; inspect her as she lies beetle-helpless before me: the flannel over her privates, pearls still round her neck, Palmolive balanced on her chest. Through half-shut eyes she seems to float in a white frock: where the sleeves end her throat is turkey-red and wrinkly. Through open eyes the white frock is her body.

Her breasts have no nipples, and I wonder who bit them off. I stare at her scant pubics, and the cobwebs under her arms; her marble legs have varicose veins, her toes lie crooked—fringed with little hairs. Her belly is a peach with a bruise of navel. I want to put my thumb in.

But it is best when she puts her head in my lap and I can get close and squeeze for the worm of pus. I make marks with my nails, and say there is a blackhead; I find ingrowns and pull out silver that didn't go blue. She says there's a lump of wax and then I have more to do—for I love all the little things best, and making dirty come clean. And she makes her chin go hard, and it looks like orange peel and my fingers come together and out comes the little dot. And the head came off the pimple and I saw blood—I really should have pricked it with a pin.

Sometimes we go out under the peach tree with Reece, and the lawn is wet from the hose and the seat is like a boat. I pluck her eyebrows where they meet by the frown and break my promise—nip along the lip. And her eyes come open and she swears, calls me bloody cow, and nearly hits me and Reece is upset—tells me to stop and her voice goes thick.

My grandmother loves her garden. She wears her hat and the shoes with the hole for her bunion. She stole a daphne cutting from a garden down the street— snipped it at night, put it in water to start a root but it wouldn't take. The same with lilac. But her fingers are green: for the broom is all threaded with yellow, and in autumn there are dahlias and the Mother's Day chrysanthemums, and fires full of leaves. And in spring the violets and hyacinths, but still she is sad about the daphne.

I waited for her to come home from town with the moist newspaper bundles that were snapdragons and marigolds and pansies. We planted them together, caught by the dusk and the moon; our fingers fumbling and touching in the mud, the smell of wetness, flies and moths zigzagging the air, lights along the street.

The sound of crickets from the ivy told us it was time to go in.

FIVE

THE front bedroom, shadowed by the verandah, was the coolest place in the house. In summer I escaped to it in my petticoat — soothed myself amongst its chilly lino daisies, lost myself in its crocheted quilt, breathed in fluff and darkness from under the bed. It was a silent room, a repository for best clothes and half-forgotten dreams. It only came alive when someone was sick.

I had measles, mumps, whooping-cough, chicken-pox, and scarlet-fever there. I lay frightened in the bed, waiting for the doctor; calming the wild dance in my chest with thoughts of the importance of the quilt that looked like a bride's veil, the candelabra with six fringed shades, the rug that could have been a sheepskin Polar bear.

Sometimes I knelt on the chair at the window; stayed there for hours: elbows out, eyes glazed — sucking and gnawing at the sill, incised already with toothy crescent moons. I looked across the redness of the verandah and the pebble-dash wall blurred by roses. I saw the rockery and the gravel, and the geraniums the colour of blood, the tinsel cinerarias and the lamb's ears. I ignored the ugliness of the gas-box, gazed past the cyclone trellis of fence — to the house across the road.

This house intrigued me. Sometimes a girl who had

the same surname as I (although she was no relation) stayed there. She could tap-dance, do the splits, walk on her hands, turn cartwheels. She showed me how to make whistles of bamboo shoots, how to suck honey from the convolvuluses.

And behind me was the room.

Beside the bed stood a dressing-table inlaid like a coat with herring-bones. It had a scalloped looking-glass and a cut-glass powder-bowl, doilies rimmed with tatting, a scent-bottle, a hand-mirror stamped with leaves.

There were matching herring-bone wardrobes. The big one held my mother's clothes. I liked to totter in her high-heeled shoes, pluck hats from their tissue-paper nests, peer into handbags — fascinated by handkerchiefs and hairpins and forgotten sixpences. I stepped inside the wardrobe — pressed my face into satin and lace and tweed, the lovely smell of Blue Grass and lavender and camphor — came out drunk.

The small wardrobe had been my father's. The thought that once his clothes instead of mine had hung there made me feel solemn. Ties and blazers and double-breasted suits that were only worn in dating photographs reproached me as I struggled into my best velvet dress. I felt guilty; the same as I did at school when we stood before the flag and remembered the Anzacs.

Nan and Reece's room was different: without mystery. The beds were draped chastely in candlewick, the chest-of-drawers and wardrobe painted white. My grandmother had a cupboard where she hoarded Vick's Vapour Rub and friar's balsam and Irish Moss Gum Jubes. In the drawer above I found slabs of chocolate, bags of liquorice allsorts and ju-jubes. Under her mattress were the confession magazines she pretended not to read.

Even the sun was kept out of the sitting-room — waylaid by shutters and curtains that reduced it to pale dapples on the sofa that swallowed handkerchiefs and pennies. There was a sideboard carved with flowers, a fire-place tiled with poppies, a carpet strewn with Paisley fern. On the mantelpiece, between two glass swans, my mother in *broderie anglaise* and I in Swiss cotton challenged Blue Boy and Red Boy reduced to china plaques on an opposite wall.

I liked the dining-room best in winter when we turned the light off and there was just the fire. We sat in a circle and the flames made the fender gleam, turned the mallee roots to faces, cast shadows on the wall. Roses bloomed in the grate; blue gum filled the room. I lay on the rug — lulled by Reece's knitting, Nan's newspaper, the murmuring wireless. In the morning my grandmother knelt stiffly in the cold before dead ashes; swept away the powder from the hearth.

I was happy in the dining-room.

I stood like a statue, my outspread arms garlanded with Reece's wool. I covered my grandmother with doilies when she fell asleep; crawled behind the tapestry front of the wireless and sang falsetto, assumed a gentleman's voice, hoping to trick someone into thinking it left on by mistake. I counted the buttons in the tin under the Singer sewing-machine decorated with gold scrolls and a silver medallion; stroked the leaves of the aspidistra beside the window.

My mother and I slept at the back in the sleepout. Bribed to bed with hot milk, stories, kisses, I waited for her. Our bed of enamel bars and brassy knobs was a cage for my animals: Koala and Camel, Pooh-Bear made from Nan's old fur coat. They protected me—with the Guardian Angel, the Sandman, the roses on the wall-paper—from the Chinaman, the Skeleton who might fall from above, the Mouse that gnawed at the wall. The mug with the chipped rim I liked to catch my lip on stood empty by the handkerchief cut from a sheet.

When my mother came I was asleep; woke, to see the eye of her cigarette blinking, finally disappearing in the dark. Then I curved leech-like to her body, lost myself in the pillow of hens' feathers.

And in the morning there is always the window and the verandah, the wall, the rockery and the bloody geraniums. Even though the girl with my name never comes, I still look. And see the girl with sausage curls and a brother who looks like a cocky and plays the flute go past.

Or I wander in the garden—popping fuchsia buds, pulling the lily-tongues (but I mustn't suck them, be-cause they're poison). I paint my lips with rose-buds and look for fairies: see them in puddles when the water splashes, climbing down snapdragons, dancing in the broken glasshouse, staring back from the well.

I have a garden at the side of the house where nothing grows but mosses, maidenhair fern, and a mysterious plant that blooms every seven years. One night my grandmother calls me, and I go out to see it covered with bells.

One day Reece helps me dress up as a bride in my night-gown and the net curtain. I pose by the fowl-house and a frieze of speckled bantams and my mother takes my photograph. She does the same when I sit without my clothes in the pink tin bath.

Then I am older.

The pink bath disappears. I pretend to swim in the claw-foot enamel one, am frightened by the chip-heater, pee down the plug-hole, am disgraced when my mother finds a tiny stool floating beside the pumice. The brass bed disappears; I watch my mother dressing when she tells me to shut my eyes: see India-rubber nipple, frizz between her legs, arse-hole dot—and am surprised.

SIX

THE KINDERGARTEN was named after the Governor's Lady. It was hidden in the back streets of Thebarton, coming dangerously close to the terraced houses of Hindmarsh and Brompton; dangerously near the maze that was Bowden—tucked behind the zig-zag railway that separated it from the upper class homes of North Adelaide, with their sandstone walls topped by plumbago and grape-vines and broken glass.

I was far from pretty blue plumbago as I walked with my grandmother through a world of concrete and cement, brick and asphalt, macadam and corrugated iron. Even the gardens looked sickly and grimed with dirt— Rose Street seemed far away.

The bulk of the gas-works loomed over everything; its scent was everywhere. It drifted through Bowden from First to Seventeenth Street; merged with the reek of the tannery by the river; mingled with the fumes that crept from the Southwark Brewery. Gas soaked the walls of houses, turned the sunlight sour, clung to my skirts, settled in my hair.

There was a Salvation Army citadel where people marched with flags and brass trumpets on Sunday. There were yards of sand and gravel and scrap metal;

advertisements for Ipana Toothpaste, Woodroofe's Lemonade, Amgoorie Tea. There was the Kindergarten with its drive lined with Norfolk Island pines.

I was quite happy the first morning until my grandmother led me to a strange lady who was the headmistress. She gave me flowers to arrange, and when I looked up from their redness Nan had gone. Abandoned —I cried. Yet, in the afternoon when she came to claim me at the gate, I was taken unawares. I had almost forgotten her.

I became a number, a name, a picture in the Kindergarten's files. The antiseptic fingers of a doctor probed and poked me. I was stood upon a pair of scales and weighed and measured; taken into a room where I was photographed without my clothes.

There was a lavatory with a row of cubicles and washbasins. I liked to sit and see how long I could pee for, listening to the other dribbles and tinkles and gurgles about me. I was happiest when I was a spy, a *voyeur*, an eavesdropper. I thought it strange to hear the boys' voices outside—how funny it would be if the wall wasn't there.

After lunch we rested. Best friends went next to each other—clasped hands and giggled before they fell asleep.

I came home and at night I could not sleep for thinking of the next day. Each morning the excitement mark on my cheek tingled, burned red.

We finger-painted, grew wheat in saucers, cut chains of figures with blunt-end scissors. We shook dewdrops onto our tongues, hunted for lucky clovers, found daisies in the lawn. We frightened ourselves on the slippery-dip, flew through the air on chains, calmed ourselves on the swing.

There was a sinister wooden tower that I watched others climb. There were books with buttoned covers and felt pages. There were dressing-up clothes, and I longed for the black and white Pierrot; the ones who climbed the tower got it first.

(I dream of the Kindergarten children still: Joan Stott, born on my birthday, who wet her pants at the Botanic Gardens; Betty and Joan Smith—the Twinnies, whom you couldn't tell apart; monkey-face Stanley Oliver, whose sister pulled out her hair; Brucey Neighbour, who lived in a house with a hedge dotted in berries I put in a matchbox; Daphne Ring, whose dress was embroidered with egg.)

Daphne became my friend. She had a skin disease that made her hands look like snakeskin gloves. One day we hid from the teacher in a cement pipe; pretended we were moths in a cocoon, rabbits in a burrow. Daphne scratched her hands, made a storm of snowflakes; she told me her father killed chickens, and the dead skin merged to feathers and I smelt blood.

I was amoral, secretive, devious: stole a milk-jug cover of net and beads; picked up other people's hankies and gave them to Reece to boil.

A girl showed me a Mickey Mouse book, and the buttoned books weren't as good. I thought of it all day. At last I crept to the cloakroom where it was—hid myself behind the rain-coats, sat cross-legged with the Wellingtons. I only thought of Mickey; the teacher who parted the coats gave me a fright.

One day I thought of my mother and longed to see

her. A bird was in my chest, stones choked my throat, needles pricked my eyes. I was hurt with wanting her. I had to go home.

I walked down the drive and up the asphalt. I didn't see the advertisement for Ipana Toothpaste. I crossed George Street by myself. I went past the gas-works and the priest's house and the grandfathers. Down the lane. And got excited up the path and in at the door and only Nan was there. I was still crying when frizzy-hair Miss Trembath came to get me—discuss me in the kitchen.

The days passed.

Suddenly it was December. I made my mother a present: stencilled a lamb all blurry onto card; stuck below it a calendar, dated 1945.

We got ready for the Christmas play. I was the tallest so I was the Angel. I wore a sheet, crêpe paper wings, and waved a star. Mary was a show-off in royal-blue.

On the last day there was a Fête with lucky dips, toffee apples, and a flute band. My grandmother and the mothers made dolls for the Christmas tree; I chose the one Joan Stott's mother made and Nan was hurt and wouldn't speak. There was a concert, and I watched a girl with curls like Shirley Temple do the tap-dance.

I had to say goodbye to the Norfolk pines, the lavatory, the black and white Pierrot; to Miss Trembath and the headmistress. Even to some of the children, for not everyone was going to the Infant School at the end of Rose Street.

THE SCENT OF EUCALYPTUS

For some there is the convent beside the Queen of Angels' Church and a blazer with badges and a lily on the pocket.

I envy them.

SEVEN

I was afraid of the dark.

(The journey up the passage is a long one. I get frightened: think I'll never reach the switch. I make it better by flapping arms and calling songs. But still the panic gets me. There could be ghosts. Sometimes I do it slower—cut a path through darkness room by room. For each room has its switch.)

With the click of the final switch I was safe. I was a magician whose finger retrieved familiar objects from the dark. The very banality of these trifles proved comforting: the table my mother called occasional with its old lady and her porcelain balloons and the urn all nymphs and criss-cross laurel; the specimen shelf bearing bunnies and a gee-gee and a weeny tea-set, and Cinderella's slipper, Robin redbreast on his rock and Venetian glass that made a shadow on the wall.

Yet the pretty things couldn't comfort me for long, because then I saw the door. Usually I didn't—usually I came in the back way to keep the carpet clean, and now—at night, I saw it—and it frightened me. So big, and twelve glass panels with wrinkles that made it strange and made me (now you're in the aquarium, silly little girl—and hurry—hurry—quick—down again—

for—gulper, wide-mouth, swallower, hatchet—will-get-you) run away.

(The journey to the lavatory is perilous. We approach it cautiously—in pairs: my grandmother and great-aunt, my mother and I.)

My mother lighted our way with matches; marking our path with a sooty trail. She seemed unaware that the shrivelled ends betrayed us, winced as I nudged her; burned her fingers. In the pool of shadow by the shed still charred from the fire, already long ago, I saw my enemy: pigtailed Chinaman—silent one who pounces. Creepy-creepy. I held my breath—tiptoed to confuse; counted the encroaching trees to calm the pigeon in my chest: furry-fingered fig, green-gloved peach, apricot and orange, quince with blotting-paper stars.

We were there.

The lavatory was different in the day-time. In the hide-and-seek summer we cried 'barleys' and collapsed on the seat in turn—heart pounding, eyes sparkling—pumping out the pee and shit as fast as we could; longing to be gone—to creep through the soursobs, breathe in the crackling blueness of the sky. Carol told Elvio, the Italian boy, to come in too—there was nothing to see but her skirt. When we were thirsty, and the tap was too far, we pulled the chain and drank from cupped hands. We had books we hid on the cistern shelf.

At night it was cosy inside: the door latched, the Chinaman vanquished, my mother close, spicy smell. There was no light-switch but the dark was friendly. I lifted the wooden lid—one last ritual to go through: listened for the mole; he was there, but he was cunning.

Once I felt his moist snout up my bottom; once, through the open door, I saw a bird — an albatross, a snow goose. I made a poem.

At night the lavatory became a confessional booth, an altar to the past. My mother told me about my father. She could not see me as she puffed at the cigarette Nan did not like her to smoke in the house. I began to cry.

My father who never was, was once a child. (The child sits dimpling on a postcard in short skirts beside a wistful little girl and three sisters. The sisters wear pudding-basin hats and flowers with silver-paper stems. The sisters are Molly and Nell and Margaret. Margaret is the child's mother.)

Margaret Collins married William Hanrahan in 1912. He was a blacksmith's striker; she was engaged in home duties. They had two children: my aunt, Kathleen, who was the wistful little girl; my father, who was christened Maurice, but called Bob. The marriage was not a happy one, and soon the parents parted; not physically at first, although the distance they travelled was great — merely emotionally (that way no one knows). She retreated from his scepticism and lusts, his alcoholic hazes and race-course cronies, to the safer world of the Mass, where she breathed a more rarefied air: perfumed by swinging censers, punctuated by tinkling bells, nourished with wine and wafer and the poetry of bleeding Jesus. Eventually the withdrawal became complete — when the children grew up she moved away for ever. Kathleen married and lived at Linden Park; Bob stayed at Dew Street with his father.

My father who never was, was once a boy. (The boy

goes on outings to the seaside in a linen suit, black stockings, a boater hat. He rides a tricycle holding a cat, marches with a kettle-drum, sits cross-legged in the Marist Brothers' photograph.)

My father won a scholarship to the Christian Brothers' College. He was sent letters of congratulation by Father Geoghyan and Miss Hocking who taught him and J. C. Stephens who trusted that the Divine Child would keep him well and shower him with all His choicest graces.

My father had a picture of the Madonna: blue robe, strawberry heart, rose garland, wicked dagger, pleats of light, limpid gaze, hooping halo. She held an Easter lily in Her hand; She lived safe in a celluloid frame and a cellophane square.

My father had a *Child's Manual of Devotion*, presented to him by his mother, bought from Pellegrini & Co., Publishers to the Holy See. (Did he peruse this Table of Movable Feasts, these Angelical Salutations and Acts of Contrition; this Litany of the Holy Name of Jesus, this Prayer to the Blessed Virgin for the conversion of England?) He had a *Garden of the Soul* printed in Dublin, blooming with Immaculate Hearts of Mary and Sacred Hearts of Jesus, listing Ember days and days of abstinence from flesh meat and Acts of Hope and Charity and Faith.

My father had a friend called Paul who wrote him letters about Scout Camps at Tanunda with chaps and capital ideas and decent swimming holes and pine-needles for a mattress; and of Leo Ryan who got one hundred in history and maths, Jack Webster, Ron O'Connor, Brownie Brazel, and Tommy Reardon.

(Where are they all now? Where is my father who wore the badge with laurel leaves and *Signum Fidei* round a purple star?)

He read of Lorna Doone from red-bound pages (and I survey now, thirty years after his death, his pencilled annotations that are the nearest I will get: *repute* means *good reputation*, *dialect* a *branch of language*, *coquettish* is *fond of flirting/flirtatious*, *eternal reaper* could be *death*), and he had bands that fastened with mother-of-pearl buttons, a bandanna fringed with silk, knotted ribbons of turquoise and grey, corded ribbons of violet and umber (all part of what uniform? — sacred or carnal?) and scout tabs, too, embroidered with: 8TH ADELAIDE (C.B.C.) (did they nest on his shoulders?) and another that said just: SOUTH AUSTRALIA (where did that go?).

I sat in the dark lavatory and wondered what happened to my father to change him from the pious child, the 'dear Maurice' of the letters. I could not equate the virtuous boy with the husband who bought friendship with my mother's thirty pounds.

(Did it happen when he failed the eyesight test for the Railways and took instead the job at Holdens that he hated? Did it happen on those long Sunday afternoons when he read of Joyful Mysteries and kicked his heels? Did it happen when the mother whose favourite he had always been, left him and went to live alone?)

Perhaps the pious child and the virtuous boy never were; just as the father never was.

(It is idle to speculate. I will never know.)

I wiped my eyes as my mother adjusted her clothing

and pulled the chain. I clasped her hand — for the path seemed longer, the darkness darker, the dining-room farther away. My mother struck a match, and we began the journey back.

EIGHT

GRANDFATHER HANRAHAN and Great-grandfather Collins lived next to each other in Dew Street. Their semi-detached cottages were separated by a small side yard. Each was joined at the spine to a red-brick twin. Grandfather Hanrahan's neighbour remained anonymous, but St. Teresa, where Great-grandfather Collins lived, drew status from being next to the priest's house. This house with its rosary-clicking stillness, its incense-laden spruce hedge was lovely.

I visited the grandfathers every Sunday.

My mother called me when it was time, took me out the gate slung with lavatory-creeper, waved me down the lane.

At the corner I turned into Dew Street and advanced slowly along the familiar Kindergarten path. Without Nan to restrain me I stooped to collect bobby-pins from the gutter and saw jelly-fish phlegm, examined initials on fences, saw a man do pee by Olricks' gate.

I passed the stuccoed turrets of Bradeys' where rhododendrons blazed on gravel; gazed longingly at the chemist's mock-Spanish villa, where once I hunted for a lost ball and peered into brushwood greenhouses, saw a bird's nest at the top of a tree. I passed the monkey-puzzle and the bamboo lane, caught the spark of sunflowers that told me I was nearly there. Came to number twenty-three and the grandfather who waited.

Once my grandfather was a slender young man in a butterfly collar who stood at the seaside with the child Bob in a linen suit, and a lady in muslin and a cartwheel hat. The lady was my grandmother. Suddenly they were all gone: Bob to the marble cemetery, my grandmother too, and the young man quite vanished with his butterfly —become a grandfather who was fat and lived alone.

My mother told me how my grandmother prophesied over my cradle like a Good Fairy that I should be too sensitive for this life; that I should have a thorny path to tread. My father was her favourite, and when he died she was heart-broken; locked herself in her room, refused to come out. She was a shadowy figure who faded early. When we went to visit at Linden Park my mother showed me the nursing-home she died in.

Linden Park had nothing to do with Dew Street. It was an outer suburb, its wide streets lined with Tudor houses and lawns and crazy-paving paths and goldfish ponds and prunus-trees.

My mother and I went out there in the tram, past the Victoria Park Race Course where Grandfather Hanrahan worked in the Tote. We met Catholic relations with Irish names: cousins, who went to schools called Star of the Sea and Loreto and the Convent of Mercy; aunties and uncles gossiping after Mass, sucking down sweet weak tea, eating Pavlova, picking out passion-fruit seeds.

There was a telephone, a latest model Vanguard, Raphael's nicest Madonna in a bedroom that smelt of sandalwood. There was a fir-tree at Christmas with glass balls and a tinsel star, a money-box nigger-boy who ate the coins, a walnut piano, a real chandelier.

They spent holidays at Victor Harbour, Port Noarlunga, and sometimes Christies Beach; they prayed to St. Anthony for things that were lost. My uncle owned two butcher shops and three racehorses. My cousins attended the flashest Catholic schools in Adelaide, and he wore a blazer with a Platignum fountain pen and red braid, and she had a felt hat and lisle stockings like Reece. I knew I wasn't as good as them.

Grandfather Hanrahan did not speak to Great-grandfather Collins. He contented himself with a wry comment about his father-in-law's peculiarities as he lifted me over the fence to the glum little housekeeper on the other side.

My mother told me that the grandfathers hated each other. She told me that one night Grandfather Hanrahan came home drunk and went into St. Teresa by mistake; climbed the curtains, pulled them down in a frenzy.

My grandfather spent most of his time in the sleepout. It was dim there, with screens of wire-netting to keep out the flies. Sometimes he was still in bed and I sat amongst the dirty sheets and explored the prickles on his red face with my fingers, and felt the soft cushions of his flannel stomach.

He whispered that we should live together always when I grew up; he would have a little housekeeper then. He gave me Tote tickets with magic numbers, a silver mug he made himself, a pink bank-book, a purple ink-pad and a rubber stamp with my name on it backwards. He gave me bags of oranges until one Sunday I got caught coming home with them by the girl from the corner: she dragged me to the air-raid shelter in the nasturtiums; took off my clothes, folded them neatly, stuck pins in me—ran away with the oranges.

When I was sick with the chicken-pox my grandfather visited me; I saw him in the doorway with a flagon of orange-cordial. He took me for walks past the Wheat-sheaf Hotel and bought me custard tarts and vanilla squares.

Then, like Charles Ebenezer and Little White Puppy and Bob before him, my grandfather disappeared. He was knocked down by a car on the Port Road after he had been drinking.

I went to the house beside St. Teresa for the last time. It was night and I was with Nan. I saw the sleepout and the sunflowers and helped lift the incinerator made from a petrol-tin onto the wheelbarrow. Nan said we might as well have it as anyone else. I felt sad as we rattled away.

Then there was only Great-grandfather Collins to visit. He was a very old man with a square head that wobbled on a thin neck and a bobbing Adam's apple. There was something serpentine about his long face mottled with age and stubble, its slit of mouth rimmed with scabs in winter, its heavy lids that flickered over rheumy eyes. He had shrivelled hands rashed with spots.

The side gate squeaked as I opened it. I plucked at the bush of southernwood; saluted the canvas water-bag that swung in the fig-tree. At the bottom of the yard past the fence and the tennis-court was the house where a girl who had something wrong with her lived: she had to hold her hanky to her mouth to stop the phlegm (she had a little sister who couldn't grow).

I thought of her and felt subdued as I stepped into the kitchen. All was as usual: the housekeeper at the sink, the dish of bread-and-milk sprinkled with sugar on the newspaper cloth, the saints brandishing their swords above NOVEMBER on the calendar, the Major Mitchell cocky in his cage. I swished through the curtains Grandfather Hanrahan had climbed, and came to my great-grandfather's room.

The blind was drawn and everything was vague. The tongue of the skirting-board licked the linoleum; the slate-grey hollow slumbered on the bed. China figurines of the Mother of God were reduced to phantoms. My great-grandfather was a waxwork figure on a horsehair sofa; his hands folded over a silhouette waistcoat. I greeted him, and lingered by the fireplace where he kept the jar of chalky peppermints stamped with crowns.

And we talked about the virtues of going to bed early, of being a Catholic; of why you should vote for the Labour Party.

I am older. Italian market-gardeners live in Grandfather Hanrahan's house — the sleepout is pulled down, cabbages grow instead of sunflowers.

I walk down the lane to see my great-grandfather. Carol comes too. She waits outside; pulls faces at Dominic and Elvio.

It is hot. The water-bag flaps on the tree; the doorknob burns my fingers. The wire door snaps crazily shut; the cocky squawks in the empty kitchen.

The dimness is exaggerated by the heat that shimmers outside and for a moment I cannot see. I step forward, grope along the passage; feel the curtain lap about me; breathe in stale perfume.

In the half-light an egg-shell shepherdess brandishes her crook; the Marys flaunt pincushion hearts. My great-grandfather is asleep—folded zigzag on the sofa.

His hand comes out to love me but I say that it is hot. He doesn't answer—just draws me close. He even hurts my arm, but doesn't seem to care. And the sofa cuts my leg and then his tongue comes out and he starts to shake. And he asks me what is under my dress. I nearly get the giggles, but then I feel scared, for my arm still hurts and he comes too close. And I tell him the petticoat and the singlet (it has a hole) and the pants of course. He smiles more then and I see spit along his mouth and more tongue and then it is really awful, because he puts his hand right up my dress and feels and a great-grandfather shouldn't do that.

I am frozen to the pearly linoleum, and then the panic comes—I pull away in fright.

He tells me he has a present for me in the fireplace. It is only chocolate; it is melting.

After that the visits stopped and I always walked past the house on the opposite side of the street. One day I saw my great-grandfather in the distance—an old man with a stick. My Auntie Kathleen said why didn't I go to see him. When he died he left St. Teresa to the Catholic Church and fifty pounds to me.

NINE

A<small>T LAST</small> it is Christmas Eve. I sit on the steps of the verandah. Behind me the house waits expectantly like an immense animal.

In the dark garden a sturdy nymph stands petrified, a fountain gushing from her hands. Then the statue moves and becomes my grandmother, one finger nozzling the hose.

I breathe in the scent of the wet earth, the drenched ferns, the sodden roses.

All about me are subdued sighs and murmurs and whispers as the garden drinks the water that slips from pebble-dash; makes the lawn a pond.

A gust of wind jumps into Nan's apron and turns the fountain to quicksilver dots. It shakes the bells in the potted fir-tree and makes them twinkle. It swings the telegraph wires, stirs the trees; swoops in at the window and laps the sill.

Lights glow along the street; beetles with transparent wings swirl with velvet moths. Crickets whirr in hedges, footsteps strike loudly. A car drones—comes nearer—the street is full of light; the verandah leaps alive and shadows stalk the wall. The car passes and the house sinks back.

Nan's voice threads the garden: calls from the hydrangea bush next door; whispers in the purple-flowering fuchsia. Footsteps slur on the gravel, and Reece's face bobs whitely like some strange blossom — swims smoothly across the lawn, detached from feet that stumble behind; hovers the rim of the fence; is swallowed by a shape that melts and merges — rises, and becomes my grandmother.

I lay in bed and vowed I would not sleep.

I thought of the endless Christmas songs played on the wireless by Auntie Peggy and Uncle Bob: 'Away in a Manger', 'I'm Dreaming of a White Christmas', 'O Come All Ye Faithful', 'Jingle Bells'. I remembered the sweating Santa Claus with the cotton-wool beard and torn trousers under his scarlet robe in the Magic Cave. I thought of Nipper and Nimble and the fairies in cheese-cloth *tutus* in the Pageant; of Carols by Candle-light, where I watched the couples kissing by the lake and got lost in the park.

I recalled the sixpences I helped Nan to sterilize; the currants and raisins and angelica, candied peel and preserved ginger she carried from the shop; the cake she let me stir, rich with treacle, figs, and twelve eggs; the plum pudding, boiled for eight hours in the damp cloth sprinkled with flour. I tried to count the jars of conserves and jellies and jams. My eyes drooped, as I remembered cauliflower piccalilli and melon chutney; ripe tomato relish and pickled onions. The last thing I saw before I slept was the empty mouth of the pillow-case that dangled above the small tent my feet made in the bed.

The pillow-case was there when I awoke — but it was fat.

I seized it greedily, and the bed wallowed in strange

objects. Sugared fish flickered in the sheets, flower-scented cachous starred my pillow, ju-jubes quivered, plaited liquorice twined. A Christmas stocking of raspberry mesh was a cage for a celluloid kewpie doll, a whistle that curled and tickled my nose, a peppermint walking-stick, a mouse with a string tail. There were three picture books and a monkey with a spotted waistcoat, a globe that filled with snow when I shook it.

The sun crept like a thief towards my booty. I pounced upon my mother and kicked her awake.

There were still more marvels to come.

The dining-room trembled with crêpe paper and tinsel, gold foil and cellophane. A spruce bough lolled in the fireplace, angel's hair floated from the curtain-rod; there was plastic holly in the lucky heather vases.

The oval table, transformed by the damask cloth, mirrored the rainbow streamers in the glitters and gleams of the best cutlery, the cut-glass cake-stand, the harvest festival dinner-set. We sat about it, sweltering in our Sunday clothes; at last Nan swept in red-faced in her pearls to release us from awful anticipation. And the great turkey with its glazed toffee hump became small and fell in pale slices onto our plates, and there were potatoes and parsnips and mint sauce and peas and a river of tomato gravy.

We ate it all, and there was Woodroofe's Lemonade and Schweppes' Lime Juice, a pudding with sixpences that remained elusive, a cake with icing-sugar and coconut and a holly sprig and a paper frill, cups of tea. We stumbled away: to lavatory, bathroom, bedroom. We banished the sun with drawn blinds and curtains; slept in our petticoats.

The summer drifts on, and Nan outwits it with cucumber peel stuck to her forehead, home-made lemon-cordial, heart-shaped Fiji fan; with lettuce like mermaid's hair, condensed milk mayonnaise, Narcissus Blancmange, Dainty Chocolate Mould, Delicious Hawaiian Cake.

The iceman becomes important.

I wait for him to come round the corner with his cabbage-leaf hat, nose hung with an icicle, sad-eared horse. I cry 'Ice-o!' with the others, and dance after his cart and the wet trail of drips it leaves behind; watch him juggle the blocks from house to house; crow when he smashes one to shivers and gives us each a piece.

The sun is everywhere.

It is in the garden: peering huge-eyed over the berry bush, roosting behind the chimney, floating like a fried egg in puddles. It mocks me when I burn my bare feet on the earth and scorch my fingers on the iron fence. It peels my nose to jigsaw patches, gilds my skin with freckles, turns the hair on my arms to gold.

It is in the house: spangling the passage with leopard spots, turning the sheepskin rug tawny, casting zebra stripes through the shutters. It curdles the milk, melts the butter, shows the dust, fades the curtains. It steals into vases and drinks their water; creeps up the cold tap and turns it into hot.

In the evening, after tea, we carried the cane chairs and the wireless with the long cord onto the lawn; sat under the fig-tree in the twilight.

(The sun hangs suspended in O'Briens' almond-tree like a tennis-ball, then lobs behind the lemon, sinks into the flowering quince. For an instant the garden blazes coldly with ruddy flowers; then geraniums, zinnias, and marigolds disappear. The moon comes into the sky; a butterfly skims the grass. The garden blooms again with pale stocks, nicotiana, sweet rocket.)

Nan shivered and fiddled with the wireless knob. We listened to the 'Australian Amateur Hour'. And complained about the mosquitoes; forgot the moon.

TEN

FEBRUARY came.

The secateurs clicked in the lily-bed, and heralded the demise of the nerine, the Madonna, and the spotted tiger. The rose mourned and flecked the earth. The wall was embroidered with climbing-geranium and ivy. There were dahlias and snail trails in the garden.

I walked to the Infant School on the corner.

It was separated from the street by a picket fence and a line of jacarandas. As I walked towards the trees they merged to a blue umbrella.

Beyond the picket fence and the trees was the red-brick school slit with eyes of classrooms and a wide-mouthed door. I only entered this door once, and that was on the day my grandmother took me to enrol.

After that I went in at the side gate.

This gate was approached by a gravel lane, that once past it forked and became two lanes. The right fork was stunted and led to a rickety building that housed the Sno-Whyte Bag Laundry, and a room above where the floor trembled and the dust swirled as a brass band practised on Sundays, and the Technical School girls did gymnasium during the week. With the left fork the little lane became a big lane that divided the yards of the houses with odd numbers in Rose Street from those with even numbers on the Henley Beach Road.

All the streets had their lanes.

Ours was friendly with nettles and the manure Nan collected in a bag. There was a wood yard and a coopery where timber sky-scrapers were turned into barrels and sawdust. There were yards that served as cemeteries for bindweed and soursobs, broken staves and the reek of wine.

The lane by the side gate was different. The grass was matted—dank with rain in winter, thick with dust in summer. Tins and newspapers skulked in the boles of trees. Drifts of oyster-shells were remnants of some sinister paper-chase below walls sprouting jags of glass and prickly wire. It was the lair of boys with Argyll pullovers and brilliantined hair.

I was saved from the lane by the gate. I crossed the asphalt yard; climbed the two cement steps, and went through the cloakroom that smelt of Phenyle and carbolic; entered the classroom that was a duplicate of the one I entered at Kindergarten.

There were the same friezes of alphabet letters and nursery-rhymes, the same saucers of cotton-wool wheat ranged along the sill, the same bulbs torn by fresh green spears, the same tables hung with hessian book-bags, the same pickle-jars full of the same tired daisies and snapdragons.

I met another headmistress, who with her soft swan's bosom and pepper-and-salt hair might have been the same headmistress I met before. But her name was Miss Hecker, and when I saw her approaching me at the end of a corridor, I muttered as the other children muttered: 'Miss Hecker, double-decker, policeman came and tried to get her,' and she was diminished.

I met another teacher, and Miss Trembath with her shivery-grass hair was replaced by Miss Traegar and a rain of hairpins that peppered our primers. And as she gathered them we peeped through our eye-lashes down the neck of her dress and saw the white doves that nestled there.

We learned to count to the click of beads on counting-frames. We learned to draw a pig from circles and a stick-man with a little hat. We sang 'Birdies are Nesting for 'tis Spring-time' and 'I Had a Little Nut-tree' and 'Where are You Going to, My Pretty Maid?'

We drew wavering lines that should have been straight, and looped rick-rack patterns with wax crayons on sheets of butcher's paper; ravaged the pages of exercise books with HB pencils that deteriorated from slender candles to pock-marked stubs; wrote a diary of all the things that happened to us and were not allowed to rub out.

We read, and there was Dot who sat in the sun, Brer Rabbit and the Tar Baby, the crooked man who walked the crooked mile. It was a race to see who could finish their primer first, and I stayed behind after school and read to the teacher; when I finished a page she stamped it and a swallow hovered in the margin.

There were other rewards for good work.

There were red ticks and gummed-paper stars and early minutes; there were scraps embossed with violets, kittens in baskets and angels dreaming on scalloped clouds.

We charted our heights against the door and I was still the tallest girl. We clasped hands in ungainly ring-a-rosies and flopped to the floor in a welter of printed frocks and serge trousers, and the boys sniggered because they saw our pants. We disarranged the minute sand-tray world where sheep and cows of lead grazed in tissue-paper meadows and a plastic swan floated on a looking-glass lake. We lined up before the doctor who jabbed us with a needle because there was a Polio Epidemic; and many children stayed away from school, and some came back changed, and wobbled with a leg in irons.

Each day at twelve o'clock, when the Queen of Angels' bells pealed and the factory siren wailed, I ate my lunch with the others. In summer we sat under the jacaranda-trees; in winter we huddled in the draughty shelter shed while the rain pounded and wept from the eaves. Nan wrapped vine leaves and waxed-paper around the sandwiches I brought in a dog-eared bag. Some children brought theirs wrapped in newspaper, and some had coins knotted in the corners of their handkerchiefs to buy pale-bottomed pies that bled tomato sauce at every bite and finger-buns specked with raisins that looked like flies. My sandwiches were always of fritz and tomato; I exchanged them for others filled with sulphur-yellow pickles and beetroot that stained the bread purple. I had Arnott's Nursery-rhyme and Menz Yo-Yo biscuits and an orange to eat too, but I longed for sherbet suckers and chew-chew bars and honey bears from the Daisy Dell Milk Bar across the road.

There were gum-trees at the side of the school by the lane, and we collected the fallen nuts and threaded them into necklaces on loops of cotton. There were forbidden playgrounds that were battle-grounds where tennis-balls and footballs fell from the sky; where the big Primary children played with skipping-ropes and hula-hoops, knuckle-bones and marbles.

I gazed past the taps and troughs, the shelter shed and the lavatories, the bicycle racks and pepper-trees and watched the girls from the Technical School, who were bigger than my mother, stream across the yard like chattering magpies—with breasts beneath their box-pleated tunics, banister-legs ending in childish white socks. I got to school early and saw the Grade Three girls jump over their Globite cases before they marched into school. They seemed impossibly old and important.

And then Lower One became Upper Two. And there were other teachers and other classrooms, other Break-up Days and other Christmases.

And then once again it was the last day, and that time I was Mary, and cradled the celluloid baby before the mothers and my grandmother in the Thebarton Town Hall.

And what did I learn in those Infant School years?

I learned to read and write and spell and count. But more than that, I came to know other children and myself. And I found that other children could be cruel and cunning and a thousand years old. I found that I must provide myself with some kind of armour, and so I became wary and learned from them—and was divided into two.

I was the one who wandered in the garden and talked with the flowers; I was the one who raced with the others across the asphalt and limped home with bloodied knees.

THE SCENT OF EUCALYPTUS

And as I grew older I became adept at leaping quick-silver from one of my selves to the other. And as I grew older the split grew deeper, yet I forgot that it was there.

ELEVEN

ANOTHER summer came, bringing with it school holidays, roses in the gardens, sprinklers on the lawns, crackle of heat in the early-morning air, blue sky swallowing me up.

I clasped Nan's hand as we walked down Rose Street. Floating above the trees I saw the cut-paper outline of the city—its spires and towers jostled by ugly shoe-box shapes. Behind it, like a cardboard stage-set, were the mauve hills of the Mount Lofty Ranges.

(Adelaide, built on the banks of the River Torrens, lies between these hills and the sea. It is a square city, girdled by a green belt of parklands that turns rusty in summer, and divides it from endless blocks of suburbs.)

So we hurried towards the hills, then turned from the grandfathers to the other end of Dew Street. We walked past the sinister lane that was no longer sinister with Nan beside me; came to the Henley Beach Road, where we sank onto the slatted seat outside Hook the boot-maker's and waited for the tram.

Which one would it be?—open-ended fury with the striped blind that careered round the corner from Hilton; or the double one that swept up grandly from the beach, bringing with it whiffs of seaweed, and tired mothers and children trailing spades and drifts of sand?

Once when I clambered onto the platform of the tram

from Henley its doors swung shut before I was properly on. My grandmother told me that I could have been killed if she had not pulled the cord. When it came, and we rose from the white seat, I was careful to hop on gingerly first, with Nan close behind like a thickly-padded bolster.

Off went the tram.

As it passed the grocery on the corner that smelt of cheese and string and biscuits, I saw the acned delivery boy, no longer clumsy, pirouetting on the pedal of his bicycle — a grey-flannel leg gracefully skimming the bar. I saw the butcher's shop with the marbled joints stuck with plastic parsley where the stout butcher trod the sawdust floor in his apron flecked with blood, and grieved for his son who had become a priest. We passed the drapery with its limp winceyette night-dresses, where a lady-assistant in a sunray-pleated skirt sold doilies stamped with arching rose-trellises. I saw the greengrocer's that marked the seasons, the Italian milk bar where I went on Sundays with the billy-can, the Greek fish and chip shop with its NOW FRYING notice in the window.

The conductor rattled his bag and took Nan's shilling; gave me our tickets and the change. We flew over Bakewell Bridge, and I pressed against the window to see the trains I heard hooting in the night reduced to toys, and the cows nuzzling the parklands we crossed to reach the cemetery. We passed the High School, then veered towards Currie Street and the fumes of the Rosella Sauce factory; sped past the green handkerchief of Light Square, and the Iceworks I always shut my eyes at, where my mother threatened to leave me if I misbehaved. Then the tram stopped with a jerk, and we shuffled with all the others; clambered stiffly into the floating confetti of used tickets beside the bank with the wedding-cake façade.

We turned into King William Street, and over my shoulder I saw we had been followed by the hills. They were bigger now, yet still blurred and distant—dwarfed by the clock-tower and cupola of the grimy Town Hall where the City Fathers plotted, where they held the *Messiah* every Christmas, where the big girls at school sang in white dresses in the Thousand Voices' Choir.

We hurried on, then paused to sniff the spiciness of moss from the florist's by the arcade, and Nan stroked the drooping heads of pansies; admired the artistic window-display of eucalyptus branches sprayed gold. We crossed the road, and I remembered to look to the left—look to the right, as Uncle Dick told us on the wireless on 'Kangaroos on Parade'; blinked, as we stepped into the shadow of iron verandahs; stopped, as Nan nipped into the Country Provisional Stores to get some of their cheese. The traffic lights changed, and we were there with all the others—under the clock, on the Beehive Corner.

We gazed at Parma Violet creams, rum-flavoured truffles, silver cachous, and crystallized rose-petals (there is no beehive). At last Nan succumbed, went in and came out guiltily with a bag of her favourite chocolate roughs. (She loved chocolate: boxes of Black Magic and bars of Old Gold are hidden in her bedroom, once she ate an Easter-egg I was given and was sick; yet still her eyes turn dreamy and her voice drops away as she tells me of the chocolates she ate before the War.)

THE SCENT OF EUCALYPTUS

All I remembered of the War was marching in a practice-line to the Kindergarten shelter; standing important by the front gate and telling a girl who trailed case in hand as usual that there was no school because it had ended. Yet the War surrounded me still: in the sheets made from parachute silk, the necklace of seeds Joan Stott's father brought from New Guinea, the games we played with the dusty gas-mask, the nasturtium-draped mound that marked the air-raid shelter in the garden. I saw still, the figures of uniformed heroes and lovely ladies that danced blackly on the windows of the Air Force building. (The dead are all about: they walk resurrected wearing Returned Servicemen's League badges in their lapels at the Anzac Day march I watch in the rain; they sit disguised in dressing-gowns and slippers, with rugs over their knees, on the verandah of the Hospital by the sea; they mock on Remembrance Day from scarlet poppy-faces in the middle of tiny crosses—as we pay our threepence and climb the ladder to see the carpet of flowers the ladies of society have sown beside the War Memorial.)

The Beehive Corner was Adelaide's unofficial meeting-place. On Saturday nights it was crowded with nervous girls in net and satin ballerinas, rhinestone necklaces and fur-fabric capes; with legs freshly-shaven, corsages of violets pinned to their collars, they waited—off to the Palais de Danse. During the day a coy mass of ladies in gloves and hats and white shoes took their place, each with a straw shopping-basket stitched with raffia flowers over one arm; each passing the time by studying other ladies doing the same.

I was proud of my grandmother, oddly upright

from the embrace of stays that fastened with spiteful teeth.

As soon as we got home she flung them off, having one of her hot flushes from the relief of it; calling out to Reece to put the kettle on. Then, as she blew on the tea in her saucer, rested her feet on Reece's knees, swallowed C.P.S. cheese spread on slices of malt loaf, she was her familiar self: collapsed in her pink petticoat, the bruise of her navel quivering, one shoulder-strap fastened with a safety pin.

On the corner, sweating in navy tussore, hair tightly curled, mouth square with lipstick flaking at the corners, petal-hat pinned high, marcasite elephants trotting across her breast, pearls about her throat, she intimidated me. She kept peeping to see if her stocking seams were straight; remembered to tuck the lacy handkerchief up her sleeve, hitch the gold watch that kept falling down her wrist.

My mother came to claim us. She pounced, surprising us from our reverie—pulled Nan's coat straight on her shoulders, fussed at her hair under the petal-hat, made clicking noises with her tongue as the handkerchief began its inevitable descent. She was a stranger from a land of Advertising Departments, block-makers, fashion board, jars of Process Black and Poster White. She smelt of Blue Grass mixed with pencil shavings.

Then we were off in a tight knot down Rundle Street, and I saw brooches shaped like bows, blouses with cross-stitch love-birds, rabbits with their legs apart—all bloody pink and blue tissue. I saw a wooden family sitting on wooden chairs and Noah and his ark and a fur coat small enough to fit me. My mother exclaimed over a dress of silk and velvet ribbons and there was a glass peacock and the lady behind the counter was old and wrinkled.

We entered Balfour's Cake Shop, ignoring trays of éclairs and lamingtons; climbed the stairs to the Tea Rooms and the waitresses in butterfly caps; sat down to our fish dinner.

TWELVE

CAROL was my friend. She lived next door but one in a house full of cats, with a mother and father, two sisters and a brother.

Carol's mother had a romantic name: Ruby Rose. A photograph on the mantelpiece showed that she was once a romantic young lady with hair she could sit on. By the time she was Carol's mother, the lady masqueraded as a woman with a creased red face, eyes fixed in a perpetual squint. A grey skull-cap was all that was left of the famous hair. She wore a fur toque shaped like a muff, ankle-socks, a much-stained apron. Her dentures clicked angrily when she talked, and echoed her words. Each night after tea her face turned monkeyish as she discarded her teeth to suck her gums.

Carol's father looked like her grandfather. Once he was a young man who came to Australia with a London taxi. The young man became that other whom Mrs. O'Brien next door called 'a dirty old man'. His nose was pitted and swollen like a monstrous strawberry. He had pale eyes embedded in tired flesh, hair in his nostrils, ears hung with pendulous lobes. Like his wife he assumed a comforting disguise: a shiny black suit, a waistcoat mottled with food and a watch-chain, slippers full of holes, a celluloid collar.

The house was pervaded with a curious musky odour

—raw and coarse, sweet and fusty. It crept into the sausages placed at every door to swallow the draughts. It had long since seeped into flaking paintwork and walls sprigged with grease spots and damp. It was most marked in the room where Carol slept with her mother.

Here it was perpetual evening. What little light penetrated the fern-hung verandah was smothered by tightly-drawn curtains. The muskiness mingled oddly with the reek of stale urine from the chamber-pot under the bed. Humped shadows were cast on the walls by discarded clothes. There was a sewing-machine even older than ours, rag rugs, old-fashioned furniture, a crazy patchwork quilt.

The quilt was made of every sort of material. Carol and I sprawled on it happily—unmindful of the premature twilight, the urine, the brooding shadows. We plotted the wanderings of a piece of apple-green silk that conjured up visions of garden parties and sunshades and spring afternoons; sniffed greedily at snippets of embossed velvet impregnated with the wistful ghosts of Parma violets and patchouli. There was spotted navy and white satinette that evoked waxed cherries and chip-straw hats; squares of red serge that signalled feverishly to dark blue flannel. I was fond of a wobbly brocade diamond; while Carol claimed as hers, a triangle of imperial purple.

Ida and Maisie were Carol's sisters. Older than she, they had a room of their own that I envied. The walls were papered with film star pin-ups from old *Photoplays* and *Women's Weeklys*—Clark Gable and Franchot Tone smouldered upon their narrow beds. Crumpled ribbons, bottles of Mystère perfume, hair-grips, and dirty powder-puffs were scattered on the dressing-table; a koala bear and a doll dressed as a bride sprawled abandonedly in a corner.

Ida was adenoidal, with a deep voice and myopic eyes; Maisie resembled the romantic young lady in the photograph. Ida's hair was combed forward over one eye in parody of Veronica Lake; Maisie's tangled in uneasy imitation of Rita Hayworth. They both wore puff-sleeved dresses with elastic bodices, charm bracelets, and ankle-strap shoes. Soon Carol was able to boast of Maisie's diamond engagement-ring. My grandmother and Mrs. O'Brien were at their front fences the Sunday the fiancé came to visit. Nan whispered that he looked something like Van Johnson, only shorter.

Ronald was Carol's brother. He shared a room with his father. They slept on identical camp-beds and peed into the same china pot. The room was full of crystal sets and ear-phones furred with dust, broken wirelesses, yellowing newspapers, flannel underwear. Ronald, at thirty, had cocooned himself securely in khaki apathy. He was a clockwork man who turned the corner into Rose Street each workaday evening at half past five— except Friday, when he got drunk before the pubs closed. He reminded me of a ventriloquist's doll, with his round face and polished hair, his dull eyes and bobbing khaki shoulders.

At night everyone crowded into the front room around the red chenille table. Carol's father presided at one end over tobacco-tin and pipe cleaners. The smoke from his pipe spiralled towards the ceiling and the faded garlands of paper chains that hung there from one Christmas to the next. Carol's mother worked opposite at her latest quilt, scraps of cloth flecking her lap, gums tirelessly pacing her dancing needle.

In the front room, at five o'clock every evening, Carol and I listened breathlessly to the latest episode of 'Superman' on the wireless. Here we played Ludo, Happy Families, and Fish; built houses of playing-cards and pondered the intricacies of jigsaws. We had drawing competitions, with Carol's mother — who celebrated her artistry with a study of indelible-pencil gum leaves in a plastic frame — acting as the judge.

Curled up at our feet were any number of cats and their latest offspring. There were legions of them: ginger and tortoise-shell, roan and smoky-grey. Their smell mingled with all the others in the house; the back verandah was dotted with neat piles of excreta and saucers of stale milk. Ronald shed his apathy, and whistled as he drowned the new-born kittens in a bucket under the peach-tree, but paradoxically they still multiplied. Carol had her favourites: Velvet and Diamond and Star. She plucked the fleas from their ragged coats, soothed their torn ears and bleeding paws, gorged them with morsels from her dinner. I could not tell them apart.

We played on the back verandah when it was wet, with an assortment of balding plush toys. The cats romped about us, capsizing the saucers of milk, sharpening their claws on a silent German piano that looked as incongruous on the uneven brick floor as the London taxi did, abandoned to the nettles and rain in its hessian and iron shelter. In winter the verandah was webbed with clothes-lines — drops of water fell coldly on our heads from crutchless bloomers, snot-rimmed hand-kerchiefs, greasy tea-towels.

Here, too, Carol washed her hair in a chipped enamel bowl, and grimaced and shrieked as her mother combed its tangles. Then I was jealous; for with the shrieking over, and the dirty water emptied down the drain, she was a princess. Her hair, spread in crinkles over her shoulders, challenged, and matched, the sun. I felt better when it became two thin braids, and Carol was her goose-girl self.

The verandah kept watch over a tiny kitchen painted electric-green. The mélange of smells grew stranger: musk and urine and cats vied with coffee essence and cabbage and fish. On torn oilcloth, like an arrangement of holy relics, stood the tomato sauce and vinegar, plum jam and condensed milk that accompanied every meal— their glass and metal sides tattooed with congealing stigmatas. Disregarding the protests of mother and grandmother, clutching knife and fork and plateful of cooling food, I hastened to the kitchen whenever I could, to eat with my friend—drawn from cut-glass and damask proprieties by its feckless glamour.

In the yard full of weeds and dust and blistered earth we jumped ropes, bounced balls, traced whorls and emblems in the swirling dust. Sometimes we found witchetty grubs in the pile of mallee roots by the door and contemplated toasting them—they were saved by their very helplessness.

Beside the water tank and the patch of rhubarb and a shrivelled little lemon-tree was a lavatory where we sat and meditated upon the newspaper squares that hung from a spiked hook. At the side of the lavatory, where the ground was mossy and slug-green, was another lavatory, long abandoned, that Carol's father made for her when she was small. This wooden box with its evil hole proved unaccountably intriguing; I peered into it often, in the hope of discerning some ancient souvenir of my friend's carnality.

The minute front garden was choked with roses. Coral suckers hooped above mildewed leaves, neglected petals quivered with sap-green aphides. Nan's pink Lorraine Lees looked vulgar and over-blown beside the tissue-paper frailty of queerer red and white.

We sat on the verandah on summer evenings, behind the swaying screen of bridesmaid's fern and a hedge of rosemary; crooning sentimental songs from *Boomerang Songsters*, and telling secrets. And Carol told me that she would become a spangled lady in a circus; would swing from the high trapeze, and stand on one leg on the back of a coal-black stallion. And I believed her.

(How are we to know that already Carol's future has claimed her?—that she will live out her life in Rose Street: in the house with the silent piano, the patchwork quilt, and the cats; in the yard with the rusting taxi, the witchetty grubs, and the moss?—that her future will lead no farther than the Cowandilla Road, where she will tread five days a week to wear out her nails at a battered Remington?—that she will sit on alone at night, shorn of all the secret radiance that slumbered in her pigtails; imprisoned by a television screen and the fern and the red and white roses and her family? How are we to know that she is closer now—dreaming on the verandah of the spangled circus life—than she ever will be, to reality?)

THE SCENT OF EUCALYPTUS

Anything seemed possible on the verandah, and so we parted easily, waiting impatiently for the next day to come.

When it does, we will awake and escape to our backyards; and I will climb the apricot, and Carol will climb the peach; and we will wave and coo-ee to each other, and be Tarzans.

THIRTEEN

I AM A city child. At night I am lulled to sleep by the owl-hoot of last trains; see the cold lights of planes stub the stars. By day I am bound by the fickle winks of amber, green, and red at corners; walk to school over earth I cannot see beneath a concrete crust.

I see the earth spinning like an aniseed ball in space — covered with a brittle casing of mortar; hammered by a ceaseless rain of cigarette packets, sweet papers, chewing-gum, dog shit, and gobs of yellow phlegm. This is my nightmare — when the noise of cars crowds out the nightjar; when I am strangled by telegraph wires, smothered by the gas-works' stench.

Yet there are rainbow patches in my concrete quilt. And at night in my sleepout, perched between the cement verandah and the chocolate earth, I hear the train whistles blend with the cries of cats; and sleep to the scent of stocks and lilies nurtured by the moon. I wake to a chorus of roosters, and the derisive hoot of an unlikely kookaburra; and the eye of the sun mocks the tinsel memory of the traffic lights.

I am a city child. I am bound by a tram-line to the city minutes away; to the parklands and clock-towers, the chimneys and flagpoles; to the Beehive Corner and Balfour's.

But the city is an island surrounded by hills and sea.

And one day I cross the road, and stare at Hook the bootmaker's from the other side, and see that the silver ribbons stretch in another direction too.

They nibble, as surely as Nan's sewing-machine, through the cement—away from the city, towards the sea and the sand and the tired mothers I see returning with red-faced children; towards the Gulf of St. Vincent that laps the boot that kicks at Kangaroo Island in the atlas; towards the blue that is the Indian Ocean, edged with the names of seaside towns that sound of England and poetry: Semaphore and Tennyson, Grange and Henley, Glenelg and Brighton, Seacliff and Marino Rocks.

And then I was on the tram, and it sailed down the Beach Road towards the Plaza Picture Theatre, collecting passengers at every stop. We left St. Ives behind, and raced market-gardens blooming with cabbages and crouching figures, jungles of bamboo and lanes of beans, roadside stalls where Italian women with faces like the Madonna and handkerchiefs round their heads sold gladioli and tomatoes, red-brick houses waiting to blaze with Virginia creeper, and the Kooyonga Golf Links where retired executives meditated over bright green grass. Then the tram lurched and stumbled over a bridge, and I saw the river coiled beneath us; watched it—smaller, thread oily marshlands. And then the tram went faster, the back-yards pressed closer, and we peered unashamedly at asbestos bungalows and ragged gardens choked with alyssum, lobelia, and orange marigolds—tufted French ones and frilly pompon giants. And we surveyed coldly, rotting bicycles and wash-tubs hidden on roof-tops, fowl-houses improvised from bed-steads, limp clothes-lines strung with bathing suits.

Suddenly I caught my breath, leaned forward — and sure enough, caught a glimpse of leaping blue. And lost it behind a hill of tamarisks. Then, as we rounded another hill, before us appeared a basinful of sea, brimming and lurching a pale rim. As the tram surged down Seaview Road, the blueness was everywhere, and so bright that my eyes pricked with pins — I looked away. Then we stopped with a shudder; got off at Main Street, and there were people all about — chattering and gleaming like satiny monkeys, smelling of salt and ice-cream and sun-tan oil.

We walked down to the Esplanade and its row of boarding-houses called Laurel Mount and Coastal Court, The Anchorage and Green Lawns; each house guarded by a stone wall carpeted in purple noon-flower; each front garden rampant with identical clumps of red-hot pokers and hydrangeas and Iceland poppy borders.

We went on: turned our backs on Laurel Mount and crossed the road, passed under a horseshoe of fairy-lights snuffed out by the day, mounted the blunt-nosed jetty. And as I held Nan's hand tighter and looked about me, it seemed that there were two beaches.

Behind us was Peter Pan's Playground where the merry-go-round horses pranced on barley-sugar columns and the Grand Dipper curve sliced the sky. There was the notice warning: 438 PERSONS WERE TREATED FOR CUT FEET LAST YEAR — TAKE CARE, the kiosk that sold ice-cream dandies and Bush biscuits, the stalls dealing in peppermint rock and saveloys. There were the twin fortune-teller booths hung with testimonials and film star photographs and enlargements of letters from England and the Queen, where Madame Alicia and Gipsy Rosalee waited to prophesy on grubby velvet cushions.

There was that beach — where water spurted from dolphins' mouths, and fluted lamp-posts were smothered in geraniums, and the brilliance of sunken gardens was doused by the crumpled faces of old-age pensioners.

And all about us, breaking the magpie chatter and overwhelming it, was the measured fading and falling of the waves on another beach far below. I gazed out at a sea that broke in splinters upon black rocks and licked feverishly at a buff half-moon of distant sand. I peered through the chinks in the creaking planks at my feet, and it sprang strangely close. I heard it slap tarred piles starred with barnacles; I saw it swallow bootlace weed and wrack, sport with a shoal of swimmers and a flotilla of little boats that skimmed its face.

And on the buff sand, dwarfed by all that reassuring splendour, mesmerized by the sun, were tiny people and scattered tents — pale blue, lemon, orange, and white. Strewn about the people and the tents were seaweed and pyramids of clothes, sun-umbrellas that looked like bent-stemmed flowers and more tiny people in deck-chairs.

Then without warning, the sky clouded over; the sea was flecked with rain. The sand was flecked too, and all the people disappeared: through the flap-mouths of tents, under the jetty, into the sea. Nan and I sheltered with the others beside the kiosk, and soon only forgotten clothes, and children frolicking in the shallows were left on the beach below.

The rain stopped; the sun came out, and Nan said it had been playing fox-in-the-grapes. The people reappeared too, my sandals squeaked in puddles—it was hotter than before.

We sat on the sand that already was dry: my grandmother, with a hat of tight felt flower-buds on her head, and the marcasite elephants pinned to her front; me, in my sun-suit and floppy bonnet. We watched leaping figures run laughing into the waves, beach photographers walking backwards in Panama hats, proudly-strutting lifesavers. There were family parties with thermos flasks and bottles of Woodroofe's under the jetty; and behind us, rows of changing sheds where other families celebrated the sun over stale newsprint. Next to us lay a stout woman in a bathing suit camouflaged with sand. She yawned languidly, scratched her head; I saw a black powder-puff shimmering with sweat.

I undressed beneath a towel, and ran over a drift of crumbling ivory which soon became wet and firm.

The water was quite warm. I danced in a clasp of seaweed; dug in my toes, and made a storm of clouded brown. I waded out further, and did wee through my bathers—felt the comforting warmness change into stinging blue. And watched a girl swim with a gold watch on her wrist; thought I saw a shark; was frightened by a head in a rubber cap. Then I swallowed a bitter draught of salt. I felt sick; my ears began to hurt. I pushed through the waves; ran out in an aching agony of shivers. Nan waited at the water's edge, her arms spread out like Jesus—caught me in the towel.

As my grandmother rubbed me dry, the stout woman

stirred; brushed away the dried sand that looked like bread-crumbs; surveyed my chest with interest. I felt unaccountably ashamed and hurried on with my clothes, remembering another outing to another beach, when I wriggled from my bathers in the room that smelt, and saw the ugly woman—all oily skin and bell-shaped breasts. And shuddered; tried to forget.

Dressed again, I tucked my skirt into my bloomers and paced the sands; was scolded when I forgot my bonnet. I played with strange children and asked them to be my friends, I dug for water and found instead shells like the moons on my finger-nails—prised them apart, and discovered wedges of pearly jelly. Nan called me: we ate tomato sandwiches sprinkled with sand; I sucked at an orange, she sighed for a cup of tea.

(The tide comes in, the families depart—seagull scavengers take their place. The sea lingers on the deserted sands, slowly creeping towards the caves under the Esplanade. It sucks away one by one the sand castles stuck with cockles and Venus shells. It gorges itself on silver-paper, orange peel and newspapers; leaving in their stead pebbles veined with marble, driftwood, an old boot, sausages of jelly-fish, sea-gooseberries and dead men's fingers.)

It was time to go back to the tram stop. I dragged my feet as we shuffled through the sand behind the blurred voices of anonymous others. I grasped my bucket of shells and felt sad as the whisper of the ruffled sea grew fainter. We left Peter Pan's Playground, now ablaze like some lurid Hell. We left the criss-cross jetty and the line of lamp-posts, each topped already with a rosy moon. We left the dolphins' mouths and the old-age pensioners, Madame Alicia and Gipsy Rosalee. And I felt sad.

I felt better when we reached the stop, for I saw we stood outside the house I remembered from the year before, with a garden that merged in stained glass fuzziness. On a stone toadstool, beside a gnome and a windmill with motionless sails, a petrified girl proffered frozen roses.

I was admiring her when the tram arrived.

I forgot her and the sea and everything else as I sank into the seat. And fell asleep.

FOURTEEN

AUNT POLL and Uncle Will lived in the hills.

I remember rising while it was still dark to visit them; dressing, half asleep, in the warm kitchen; gazing through the early-morning twilight at the moon; watching the sky turn pale and frayed with light; seeing houses jump forward from the darkness; hearing the cold voices of first roosters, the kookaburra's ruffled peal.

The moon was a smudge when we got to Victoria Square; the sky was streaked with sun. Little buses waited, and seemingly at random, my grandmother chose one; we clambered on, and the other buses became unimportant — they waited for those whose destinations were not ours. Yet I deciphered their chalky markings; learned that there were names that were not Houghton that made the hills spring near.

I read: MONTACUTE, and saw its woods; INGLEWOOD, and smelt the wattle; HERMITAGE, and lost myself in a dark garden. (And there are others just as lovely: Piccadilly and Longwood; Gumeracha and Golden Glen. There are Stirling and Crafers, with their mists and dripping rains, their holly-trees and haw-

thorn—more English than England. There is Basket
Range, where it is always autumn: the sky a crumpled
ivory, the old houses cowled with creeper, the russet
apples fallen in the grass; Cherryville—a froth of lacy
bridesmaids, Mount Lofty—where we watched the
lightning from the Obelisk, Chain of Ponds—a necklace
of mottled blue.)

The bus roared off—the driver snatching lustful side-
glances at girls on bicycles. Soon we left Adelaide behind, and the asphalt of the suburbs became grass. (The
bus driver sat on a red seat. His hair was black against
a cinnamon neck; his shirt had wet patches under its
arms. A yellow towel flapped from a rail.) I saw olive-
trees and a horse and a donkey. We passed little towns
that clung to the foot-hills: just a church, a jumble of
roofs and cast-iron porches, clumps of lilies and beds of
smouldering pinks. The sky was hung with a mosquito-
net of heat; the trees stood perfectly still. The road
slipped on and on before us, threaded constantly with a
line of wavering white.

Then we were deep in the hills. The side roads
dwindled to tracks under shadowy trees. I saw sheep
dotted on a slope like the bumps in Reece's knitting. I
saw stone houses—some like Swiss chalets, some peeping through ivy curtains—half hidden in thickets and
purple valleys.

Suddenly the bus wavered dangerously close to a sea
of rippling leaves. The crisp waves whispered all about
us; we faltered, then hurried on. And were pursued by a
restless company of the stone houses. I saw fowls pecking under almond-trees, and far away the humps of other

hills flung with paddocks: silver and sage, mustard and yellow-green.

We passed iron gateways; a face at a window; children's fingers waving us on. Someone behind us put on perfume, and the bus was flooded with sweet voluptuous scent. Nan complained about the curve and said she felt sick.

Aunt Poll and Uncle Will met us at the bus stop; we walked with them through the eucalyptuses to the house with the balcony. The house lay in a hollow; it looked like a boat amongst the glistening morocco leaves.

The golden spaniel leapt forward to greet us; I dodged Uncle Jack's prickly chin, and he looked relieved — scurried to the safety of his room and his tanks. Poll and Will told me I had grown, and called Nan 'Iris', and exclaimed over Reece. There were cups of tea to drink, and I sat on the lavatory and scattered the same grey ashes I did before. I played in the husk of an abandoned motor-car, charted the depths of the septic tank, ate a large lunch, and then it was time to walk with Uncle Will.

We followed a crooked track, and I breathed in eucalyptus and the spice of gum leaves burning far away. Faintly through the mallee came the whine of a circular saw. Close to my ear I heard the chick-oo-wee of a bellbird, the answering chirp-chirp-cherry-cherry of a honeyeater.

I saw the flash of rosellas and a black and white magpie. Uncle Will told me of the soft grey mopoke — the Boobook owl, of speckled Jack who lays chocolate-coloured eggs, of thrushes and skylarks and swallows.

(The hills are gentle, with their pale trees, their still-nesses, their drifts of smoke. Soft-bristled bushes cling to my skirt, currents of strange insects wreathe my head. There are tufted ferns, black boys, and everywhere the wattle: intensely gold, on hair-like twigs; in plumes, amongst flannel leaves; fuming in a lemon fuzz; fallen to a shrivelled crust.)

I crushed dried leaves in my hand. My feet walked over the earth, and I looked down at them and saw another world—miniature, microscopic: a rock was a hill, a crumpled leaf a plateau, a thorn a pagoda, ground-sel and twining glycerine were forests; I was a giant.

I watched ants pursue their scurry, frail stick-insects dance a gavotte, beetles stay earthbound for an instant. I saw grasshoppers, little flickering lizards, a delicate lacewing, a centipede ferociously nippered. There were secret hollows rank with the smell of mould, overgrown with brambles and toadstools. I walked over dead trails of blackberries sparked with fresh green, tiny seeds, hermit tatters of bark, twigs and mosses and fallen leaves.

(The hills are gentle, with their monotonous greys: green-grey and blue-grey, silver-grey and pink-grey. But the greys are sprigged with colour. There is the wattle, and there are chocolate lilies and honey-scented milkmaids; tinsel-lilies and spicy-leaved myrtle. There is the fringe-lily that blooms only for a day, the musky caladenia that hides under fallen trees, the spider orchid with its frilly lip. There are flowers that quilt the earth: bidgee-widgee and golden guinea-flower and lavender grevillea; clematis that climbs, apple-berry that creeps. There is the yam-daisy shaped like a dandelion; ivy-leaf violet that loves the dark, derwent speedwell and scented sundew.)

I knew other hills, too. I had seen the half-tamed slopes of Morialta Falls and Waterfall Gully, of Lobethal and Hawthorndene. I saw them when I wandered from the Sunday School picnic party; when I exchanged egg-and-spoon races and warm raspberry cordial for the cicadas, the wild flowers, and the trees. I left the picnic grounds with their see-saws and weary swings; I fled from the kiosk selling hot water, the oval, the rustic shed; I turned from the well-trodden pathway to the summit—replaced them with hawthorn and honeysuckle and brier-rose. I walked over grass dotted with rabbits' turds; I found scabs of moss, a speckled egg-shell—a creek. And waded over pebbles and ferns, my feet lapped by coldness, my fingers gemmed. I was alone with a bird's strange frog-like call. Then a twig snapped and tea-tree buds fell into the creek; my reverie and the frog-bird's melody were broken by a band of Baptist youths.

But where were the hills of the history book, stitched with the pathways of Burke and Sturt and Leichhardt?— the hills of the sun-burned earth and budgerigar grass, the azure skies and fiery mountains we sang about at school before the flag spangled with all the stars of the Southern Cross I was never sure of seeing? Where were the old dark people I did not link with the lost couples on suitcases at the railway station? Where were the crocodiles and brolgas, the billabongs and snakes? Where were the flowers that wilted in blistered clay, the rusty waves of spinifex that looped the cliff?

(The hills are gentle, their trees are pale: the scented

paperbark with its peeling trunk, the snow-white ghost-gum — warm to the touch. And prickly box that grows by rivers, silky-oak with orange flowers; blue-gum and red-gum, cider-gum and dwarf-gum; bottlebrush with tooth-brush spikes.)

I looked about me for the sunburned land. In vain.

When we get back to Rose Street with our hens' eggs and honey the trees are ugly — robbed of blossom and berries and leaves by the petulance of the season, the pruning of the Council. Sparrows sound mournfully from telegraph wires. Even the rose-buds cannot cheer me. I carry my wildflowers into the house, and already their fragrance seems fainter.

For a few days the house is full of flowers — until they wilt and shrink, drop their petals, and my grandmother complains.

(They did not look the same.)

They remind me of the shells I brought back from the beach — the shells that lost their colour once I plucked them from the sea.

FIFTEEN

I LIVED in Rose Street.

It was a long street, with a beginning and a middle and an end.

Its ending belonged to the trains and there was a Police Barracks and men in black boots and horses that did shit, and the middle had storks on one leg and lawns mowed every week, and the beginning was my street and you went past the stump tree on one side to Mrs. Dingle and the lantana hedge and the monkey-puzzle and at the end was the Italian shop and Reece got the ice-block and made me sick and round the corner the Oval and I ran across in my blue and gold stocking-cap (I had a rosette too) and got Charlie Pyatt and John Willis and John Mehaffey in biro in my book.

The part that I surveyed from afar was claimed by the trains that whistled in the night . . . the middle section led exactly nowhere . . . the other end was my street.

And I lived in a house like Anne Hathaway's on the tin (not really). It was all creamy with zigzag round the door. Red. And two funny roofs like March Hare triangles or Tudor gables (that is more romantic). And the verandah and the pebble-dash—all those little tiny stones and all rough—and snaking rose that came out pink but not called Peace (not yellow) and geraniums, agapanthus, lily, primula, fuchsia bush down the back.

A bungalow of creamy limestone with a key-pattern of bricks round the front door, it had twin roofs set one in front of the other. The back roof made the rooms high-ceilinged and cool in summer.

Next to my house were two other houses. The one with the hydrangeas where Nan's voice came out of on Christmas Eve was first of all the Carters' and Nan hated him because he called her Bluey because of her hair (the dye) and his wife Melba and Billy the baby who I saw in the bath and he had a little pink sausage in his legs—funny—and I blew his nose on the flannel and pretended once to choke him—in the lav—and I got scared when he started to cry. Then they moved to Lockleys and sent a Christmas card—Baby Jesus in the manger, and then the O'Briens came and she was fat and took me to the trots and saw a man expose himself on the Beach Road with all the kiddies passing. Dirty Pig. They gave parties and I got out of bed to watch and through the fence by the tank they were giggling and weeing by the lemon (the men) but the girls went further along. They were drunk, and made dirty jokes and sang a song. It is the beer. And poor Doogles the dog had a stroke on Guy Fawkes' and died. He looked like a rat, that dog.

The house with the field of shivery grass and the butterfly bush belonged to Mr. Willoughby the milk-man. There was a cellar that was cool and smelt like the inside of an ice-box for the milk cans and long-handled ladles. There was a stable for a cart and a brown horse that looked like a toy. Mr. Willoughby gave Reece chocolate and a rubber ball. Then he died, and the toy horse disappeared; the cellar and the stable were empty, the butterfly bush stood unpruned.

And the lady across the road looked like a golliwog. But with red hair. Or like a spider — daddy-long-legs — in her garden and there was a New Australian boarder, but not Italian, but I think Hungarian. They kill you if you are on the lawn at night in the heat-wave — Nan read it out in the paper. And he had wine that he hid in the bush at the gate when he went in. Mr. Shipp from up further did the same, but at the back, I saw with Raelene (his granddaughter) and also a bandy-leg terrier Nan said should be destroyed. White and a colour like honey and tits on its chest (naughty word) and a pinky-coloured bottom. An ugly sort of dog. There were three houses all the same and joined together — poorer houses than ours and in one the old lady was dying and didn't get many visitors — a shame Nan said, but didn't go — Italians next to them and they sit in the street in chairs and make it common. And Dot Cherry who is married but has a boy friend — a sailor boy — and we went over one hot night and looked through the fly-wire and she was doing exercises — pointing her toes, but on the bed. Really just exercises and she had red toe-nails, but saw us and chased us across the road.

Across the road, too, lived the girl I thought was a boy with her trousers and short hair, her hat with the little feather. She played cricket with us in the lane and had a sports-car and a girl friend I saw her kiss.

Then there was Nursie next to Carol and she was the District Nurse. We saw up her dress behind the roses and her legs were very fat and had garters and skin coming out over the top. It looked really rude. But good fun peeping. And she used to go and deliver babies in an Austin (it had a canvas hood) with a bag like a doctor's too. She sat in the garden at night by the hedge and the netting to keep away birds. It would be good if the birds pecked her. And then up further the girl who took the oranges and I am afraid of her but can't tell my mother. She takes her grannie's money—change from the purse —and she's blind and can't see, and that girl puts it in my sock so I'm to blame and I feel it all silvery and very cold when I stand there and she says is this all? And I don't tell my mother but in the shed she is dirty. I forget what she does—don't like to say. Horrid horrid and I can't go away—not really that bad though, but she makes me take off all my clothes one-two-three and puts fern round me and pretends to be an artist or does other things and sometimes pinches. And there is the Jacobs family that is queer and they all go along together. And Puffing Billy, something like Reece—but Nan says no. He doesn't even run but gallops with one hand tucked up like a paw and spit everywhere. And Puffing Billy is dirty-looking with eyes too close and doesn't shave but he should. He has brothers that are all right—one called the Professor he's that clever but I don't like him. They saw me up the tree. And Puffing Billy sells flags for Torrens at the football and people look and he does the bags at the Laundry. And Pearce's boy is another queer one too—white hair and has a habit he can't stop but salutes the flag up-and-down when there isn't one. Poor thing. But he said come behind the bush and show me what you've got for a penny. And I play with Carol and

David (whose father owns the wood-yard and has a dog Sam) and Dean Black whose father takes the Boys' Brigade at the Church of Christ. And Muriel Sutton who goes to St. James' Church of England School and has sisters and Chérie who does tap-dancing and says her name is French but Nan says her mother is common — as bad as Dot Cherry — had boy friends in the War. And we play hopscotch and Chérie got a ping-pong and we tried that and get stamps from the lady by the Daisy Dell. Do dress-ups and play Sevens with the ball and Muriel can do cross-arm but not too good at Number Five and collect film stars. My favourite is Esther Williams who does the swimming and I have a lovely one of her and Carol likes the one who was in *Annie Get Your Gun* (she would) and thinks she can sing 'East is East' just as well. And also 'Buttons and Bows'. Carol can do the wheel and does turn-overs on the fence and I see up her pants — she ought to change them.

We floated cigarette packets and walnut shells for boats in the rain; poked our heads under the culvert to see which came out first. We played cricket with a white ball in the dusk and frightened ourselves at hide-and-seek in the lane. We pulled the pods of itchy-powder from Borchers' carob-tree and thrust the waxy pills down people's backs. We bought newspaper parcels of fish and chips from the Greek and ate them in the gutter — sometimes had Coca-Cola too.

We heard the water sing in the culverts and knew it was winter, and our boats raced faster, and the dustman's horse stood forlorn under his hessian cape. The berries fell from the trees and rolled like marbles on the asphalt; we saw the old man from the house with the fernery skid and tumble to the pavement, saw his wife trembling like an awful puppet, and got the giggles — and felt ashamed. In November we trudged with the sagging guy, stood in Carol's garden and twirled sparklers as Catherine wheels and Roman candles dissolved away. We followed the iceman and his watery trail, watched shoals of spiralling insects round the lights, saw moons float like red balloons above bushfires in the hills.

I lived in Rose Street.

It was my street. It belonged to me, as did the O'Briens and the German lady (like a daddy-long-legs), the New Australian, Mr. Shipp and the white and honey dog, Dot Cherry and her sailor, Puffing Billy, Nursie and her secret skin, the lady who was dying, and all the others.

I only saw its ugliness, the telegraph wires and greyness when I came back from the sea and the hills. By the time the seaweed and flowers were flung away the ugliness had faded (the trees had started to grow), and Carol called for me at the gate; we went to play.

SIXTEEN

I VENTURED from Rose Street by myself.

My wanderings were random. They took me past the bloodied chop block and swirling hens' feathers in Daphne Ring's back-yard to the sanctities of Janice Budden's sitting-room where I listened to a honey-voiced crooner sing 'Down Among the Shadowy Palms', and was told it was Frank Sinatra. I was led home by the eager hand of an over-developed little girl I met in the street who alarmed me by offering to exhibit the hairs between her legs. I encountered smouldering older brothers with rose-bud mouths and spidery lashes, velvet coats, and names like Vernon or Julian in unlikely Methodist drawing-rooms. I visited the beach with another little girl and her big sister who kissed in-cessantly a youth who was just a mouth beneath a groping rug — she went to the lavatory and took off her brassière because he had broken it.

I made sorties to Maria Street to visit Joan Stott, who had a sister called P.K. after the chewing-gum. There was a harp that made silvery music in the passage, and some dusty bulrushes, and a chenille curtain. There was a house for her grannie at the back, and a playroom papered with film stars.

We sat at a table on the verandah and painted pictures

with crooked brushes while our tongues hovered wor-
riedly at our mouths. I heard the clear ping of the brush
as I swilled it against the glass, and at its signal the
water turned cloudy. My tin paint-box was full of slabs
of bright colour that changed to bitter greens and acid
yellows, turgid violets and washed-out pinks as my
picture neared completion. We had scrap albums too,
and spent long afternoons licking the sticky backs
of nigger-boys and angels, crinolined ladies and
Father Christmases we bought from the stationer at the
corner.

Joan had a cousin called Claire whom I admired, and
one day the three of us were taken by Mrs. Stott and
my grandmother to picnic in the Botanic Gardens. We
walked past the stone lions that stood guard at the gates,
and circled the pond where ducks paddled warily through
brown water blossoming with sodden bread. We saw
brick-red fish threading glooms of star-grass and crow-
foot. We walked in a dream under trees studded with
labels, past wistaria pagodas and rose arbours, hot-
houses of ferns, pools dotted with green saucers and
lily-pod cups. There were rustic bridges and sun-dials,
a Japanese tea-house and a statue of Peter Pan.

I left Rose Street to go to birthday parties that were
always the same. (See me dressed in a bunny-wool
cardigan over voile and pin-tucks proffering the requisite
parcel, all cellophane and satin ribbon, on a certain door-
step.) Once inside, there were the usual subdued children
in their best clothes; the usual proud mothers lingering
behind them. (See us eat sandwiches spread with
hundreds-and-thousands, sausage-rolls, messes of ice-
cream and liquid jelly. Witness our unconcern as we trail

from empty lemonade bottles and fruit peel and lolly papers for photographs in the garden.) When it was five o'clock we sat in an awed circle about the wireless and heard the galloping hoofs of Gandy the 5AD studio horse come closer, and Uncle Dick read the birthday messages, and revealed the hiding places of the chocolate frogs. (Come with us as we scramble in the deep grass at the bottom of the garden for our booty.)

There were birthday parties that were as predictable as the others, but different.

There were the same hundreds-and-thousands and chocolate frogs, but we ate them under the gum-trees at the Koala Bear Farm and slid down a slippery-dip that was never-ending, rode on a camel, were photographed holding a leather-snouted koala. There were outings to the Zoo where we saw the gorilla expose his private parts under a hail of peanuts; watched the poor black panther pace his cage.

I ventured from Rose Street with my grandmother.

I sat on the bed and watched as she ran about in the pink petticoat that clung to her flesh and the hard ridges of her corsets. She climbed grunting into stockings and hooked them to the pimples of her suspenders. A white cloud of talcum floated from her armpits; the familiar pearls encircled her neck. She sighed as she squeezed her bunions into too tight shoes and plucked bobby-pins from her snail-curled hair; as she slipped into best navy tussore and pinned marcasite elephants to her breast. She powdered her face with a swansdown puff, rubbed a clown dab of rouge into each cheek, smoothed her eyebrows with spit, applied discreet mascara with a little brush, painted her lips with Kiss the Blarney lipstick, put dabs of April Violets behind her ears.

We swept away in the tram, over the bridge, to the city; got off in Currie Street by the wedding-cake bank; turned into King William Street, and our exploration began.

(King William Street is slotted by Victoria Square. Here stands the dumpy monarch billowing on her pedestal, surveying her lawns, her trees, her flower-beds, her bronze heroes—Sturt and McDouall Stuart, become stay-at-homes for ever. Nearby are the dim halls of the Central Market where waxwork joints of meat jostle carnations and roses, hyacinths buried in shaggy moss, lilies and hydrangeas.) We walked past giant cheeses and slabs of marbled bacon, packets of biscuits and jars of pickles to the stall where Nan changed the *True Confessions*.

(Beyond the market and the square and Queen Victoria is South Terrace, and beyond that the inevitable parklands, the dreary wastes of landscape-gardening and bowling greens and croquet lawns. At the other end, past the department stores of Rundle Street and the Little Italy warren of Hindley, is North Terrace.

The guide-books compare it to the boulevards of Paris. Here, in a staid row, stand the baroque façades and Corinthian columns, gazebos and belvederes of the institutes of learning. Edgings of wrought-iron scallop to more miniature convulsions through long vistas of trees and lush green lawns. There are pansy and petunia borders. Between the Japanese bamboos and the veronica bushes lurks a strange company: coy Grecian ladies expose marble breasts to an impervious Matthew Flinders; Edward VII and Robert Burns keep sprightly watch outside the Library; nineteenth-century worthies muse over the University they helped to found.)

We promenaded hand in hand: past the petrified horse and rider that cavorted in remembrance of the South African War dead; down a secret alley that wound beside the ivy-draped walls of Government House with its pill-box and Union Jack. We came out by another memorial to other wars, where a great-winged angel castrated himself before privet hedges and the bloodiness of salvia.

We walked past the Public Library and a plot of grass edged with ragged palm-trees and an elongated shed that housed the skeleton that must surely have been a dinosaur's. We entered the Museum, and once again I felt lovely horror as the lions and tigers edged close with sharp white grins. I climbed the staircase to the very top, and hung over balustrades, and gazed to the bottom of the light well. I saw whales suspended in space, a wrinkled elephant, a rhinoceros, a bear. I found glass cases that lit up to reveal Willie wagtail, Robin redbreast, and speckled Jack. There were chocolate aborigines in modest loin-cloths, honey-ant men and witchetty-grub people. There was an Egyptian Room where I saw a mummy and a row of bandaged cats and a figure that looked like Reece.

We regressed to the world of 1890 when we entered the Art Gallery. Pink and silver ladies abounded, shrinking from harsh antipodean suns under parasols and trellised vine leaves. The coldness of satin gowns was matched by the chilling austerity of parquet floors. We were cowed by gold frames and too much varnish and the lizard glances of old men spangled with braid and seals and watch-chains.

(It is better if you probe a little further, for there are shearing sheds and jolly girls with ostrich plumes and Neapolitan violets; pictures with names like 'Sadder than a Single Star that Sets at Twilight in a Vale of Leaves'. There are nymphs and pipes of Pan and 'How We Lost Poor Flossie'.)

I came out with a pain in my back from all the vastness, dragging my feet. Further along the terrace were the spires of the University and the dome of the Art School, bristling with rococo cast-iron and Virginia creeper turning red. We saw art students come out with dandelion beards and skirts hemmed with safety pins. We flopped on the grass beside the pigeons and shop assistants with brown-paper lunches.

(At the far end of North Terrace, past Parliament House, is the Railway Station. Its round clock below the neon-lit Penfold's sign has hands that mark the hours jerkily, always two minutes ahead of time. There is a flight of steps specked with fairy-dust.)

Sometimes when we came back from Semaphore in the train we went out the back way, through catacombs of forgotten offices and lavatories reeking with disinfectant, where a long mirror reflected the images of prinking girls down from the country. The collection baskets of the Methodist Mission and the Sisters of Mercy, the Salvation Army and Home for the Aged were there; it was gloomy and echoing and grubby — different from the ticket offices and the chromium counter where you bought tea and yo-yo biscuits and finger-buns.

We walked past the City Baths. Across the road was the Pioneer Women's Memorial Garden; the toy cannons and clockwork soldiers, palm-trees and gravel square of the Parade Ground. Below us was the Torrens that wound up from the weir to become a tame lake where swans and row-boats and the ferry *Popeye* plied. Above our heads a pale figure in black trunks dived from the high tower, and water sprayed in an arc. On the lawns multi-coloured blossoms and buds rose to become mothers and children. Beside the *chinoiserie* bandstand, the greenness was blighted by the scarecrow shapes of metho drinkers. Far across the river, past the trees and pampas-grass, were golf-links and tennis-courts. Farther away still, was the Adelaide Oval, flecked, according to season, with flannelled cricketers or stripe-guernseyed footballers.

(And beyond the golf-links and tennis-courts and the Oval, near the apricot cathedral of St. Peter, is Montefiore Hill. Here, ringed with neatly-clipped conifers, is Colonel William Light, the Eurasian son of a Malayan princess, founder of this White Australian city. He perches high on his pink marble pedestal, and points towards the sky.)

The river wound on through rose gardens, under the elegant criss-cross of the University footbridge. It drifted to Hackney where it became a wild river lapped by reeds and parklands and the Zoological Gardens. Pine-trees shed needles and frilled brown cones under braided willows. The steep banks were encrusted with the snake-roots of Moreton Bay figs.

(At night, when the lamps on the footbridge are reflected like mother-of-pearl buttons in the river, the dark patches under the pines and the willows and the figs come alive. The mothers and children are gone, the prim paths and rustic benches belong to a tattered army of drinkers, glint-eyed *voyeurs*, and these others — betrayed by the patches of damp on their clothes, the smell of crushed leaves in their hair.)

I clasped the hand of the blue-haired lady with the pearls and marcasite elephants who was my grandmother. We walked over the pine needles and plucked the heads of silvery pampas-grass. I heard no sighs of ecstasy from the bushes, only from afar the roar of a moth-eaten lion, the wail of a caged dingo. That other world slept; its presence hinted by forlorn trails of jellyfish French letters we did not see in our innocence; the faint shadows of figures embossed upon the grass.

SEVENTEEN

T H E Primary School days slipped by like the beads on the counting-frame. They turned into weeks and months and years; marking the seasons by holidays and a change of clothes.

I still walked down the gravel lane, but now I went past the white gate, towards the laundry and the room above, where the brass band played on Sundays and the girls pranced at gymnastics during the week.

There was another white gate here, but it was bigger than the first. I walked under the elm-trees that surrounded it, past the lavatory that smelt, and the Technical building with its wooden staircase and magpie girls. Once past that and the row of taps under the verandah, I was in the Primary School yard.

I crossed the girls' playground marked with the yellow lines of the basketball court, went past the shelter shed and the bicycle racks and the furnace, the wood shed and the bell that hung from a lolling rope.

Once I heard the bell ring from afar, but now the Infant School world of the jacaranda-trees and gum-nuts, the doves that nestled in Miss Traegar's dress, the swan that floated on the looking-glass lake, and Dot in the primer was no longer mine. One day I looked across to the Infants' yard and saw Carol in my place. I called the children who sat in my classroom of the year before babies, and thought of myself as a big girl.

I was surprised at how big I was when I looked in the mirror. My legs were long, my head bobbed above the others in the marching line, yet I felt small.

(I lie in bed in the morning, and under the sheet my body coils tight: my knees reach my chin, my toes touch my bottom. I shut my eyes and whisper to myself. I want to be one with the ants—to crawl with them over the earth, to disappear under a stone. I want to wriggle through the soil with the pink earthworms; lose myself in the pointed leaves with the little pecking birds; merge with the greenness like the grasshoppers in the hills. But instead, I must be visible; walk each morning down Rose Street to the school in the short pleated skirts that show my pants.

I wear a velvet bow fastened to a bobby-pin in my hair; my socks are carefully turned over twice. I carry a bigger case than I did before. I am sorry it does not have a pink tram-pass to Lockleys or Richmond dangling from it in a leather holder. But my exercise books comfort me, covered as they should be—with the shinyside of brown paper and my name and grade in blue Swan ink and a picture in the corner. I have a wooden ruler and a pencil-case with a lid that slides off to reveal a slot for my rubber, two sections that hold pencils and a bubble-pen, a pencil-sharpener and three gold nibs. I carry my lunch in a bag although I could come home. I have a separate parcel of cake and an apple for recess, and two handkerchiefs marked with my name.)

And the days slipped slowly by. And the seasons and the classrooms and the teachers changed.

Miss White was the Grade Three teacher and I was her pet. She was gentle, with a soft cheek that smelt of powder. She had dimples, and wore dresses with buttons from neck to hem. She made me a flower monitor, and I collected the flowers the girls brought on Mondays and arranged them with one of the Twinnies in the pickle-jar vases. They were dead on Fridays — we threw them out.

When I left Grade Three I cried. I took some of my mother's drawing paper and wrote a letter to Miss White. My letter was written with a Black Magic pencil on handmade water-colour paper. It told Miss White how much I loved her.

There were no pets in Grade Four. The teacher was called Stewpot. She wore severe suits and a helmet of steely hair set in strict grey waves. She was cold, with thin lips and little eyes. She smacked our hands with a ruler and it hurt. She said we were big girls now; that we must learn. All the girls who made the error in dictation had to come forward and be slapped. It hurt. We folded our arms and sat silent when she was out of the room — Patty Briggs reported us if we talked, and there were more slaps that stung with the ruler. I was smacked when I bent my finger double to hold the pen — I could not help it, that was how it went. Because I had to hold my finger high, like an umbrella, my writing was always bad. When I had chicken-pox I stayed away from school; when I was almost better, Nan took me to a matinée at the pictures; Lorna Jones told the teacher she had seen me, and when I came back to school Stewpot said if I was well enough to go to the pictures, I was well enough to come to school. Nan was cross.

At lunch-time when the bell rang, I ran across the

playground with Catherine Oates and Janice Budden, the Twinnies and Joan Stott. We saved each other seats on the benches that made a square round each of the trees: the two pepper-trees with their herring-bone leaves and berries, the one in the middle whose white flowers looked scalloped from flannel. We sat on the benches and saved places and ate our lunches. We watched the Opportunity Class children, who looked like Reece. When we had finished eating, we drank at the taps, then played hidey and chasey and skippy; waved to the boys far away behind the furnace and the lavatories.

The playgrounds were swept by strange crazes.

Suddenly everyone was bent over a bobbing yo-yo at the end of slender string. Then there were squares of plastic filled with smaller squares and all the letters of the alphabet and one space — we moved the space about with clicks to make words. There were epidemics of skipping-ropes and rounders and rubber balls. We collected autographs and film star pictures and cards from the cereal packets. I had marbles in a draw-string bag, plastic knuckle-bones, beach bats, silkworms in a box.

One day the playground was spread with new gravel, and at recess the yard was dotted with squatting figures, moving with bent heads over the ground. We were searching for precious stones studded with glittering silver. We kept our finds that looked like teeth with fillings in matchboxes. Then the silver disappeared; the gravel was a dirty grey, and turned cruel: it tripped me when I ran after the ball, and I fell; looked up to see children who laughed at my torn knees and said they knew the colour of my pants.

And then I was in Grade Five, and this was a special class, because it was a mixture of boys and girls.

I was in Grade Five, and the other girls were Joan Stott, Janice Redway and Diana Horricks, Margaret Ettridge and Lorna Jones, Janice Budden and Rosemary Hearn. Joan Stott was born on the same day as I; Diana Horricks had a boy friend called Gilbert Perks; Lorna Jones was bossy and told me not to sniff when I had a cold; Janice Redway had white hair and eye-lashes; Janice Budden was the best runner, and had all the autographs of the West Torrens football team; Margaret Ettridge said her family had a maid, and dilated her nostrils; Rosemary Hearn was the teacher's favourite.

Frederick Harvey Goodman was our teacher. He was over six feet tall with red hair, and looked like a devil. He was a devil when he hit the boys with the wooden bat. He called them out for spelling errors and for reading comics, for chewing gum and for unfinished homework, for talking and for being late. He made them stand on the platform and touch their toes; he hit them on and on with the bat—until they cried out. He hit them, and we hid our faces so that we could not see; Rosemary Hearn and I began to cry—I felt as if I was on fire, and would burst if he did not stop.

He hit the little Grade Four boys who came in once a week. He hit Michael Saradakis who was his enemy. He hit him when he moved his hand because he did not understand that he was to keep as still as a statue. Mr. Goodman said: 'Saradakis, bend over and look at the daisies,' and he hit him longer and harder than anyone else, because he was Greek and did not understand.

And Michael Saradakis' mother came to see the head-master, but nothing happened — the beatings continued. On April Fool's Day we hid the bat, but the next day it was back — and once more we hid our faces; I began to cry.

I learned I was clever in Grade Five when I got 97½ in the exam. I learned that I was the best at drawing, and Janice Budden was the best at sport; that Rosemary Hearn had the prettiest clothes, and Ronny Morrison was my boy friend.

After lunch we assembled in the yard. All the teachers stood in a line by the shed while Miss Monk, the Grade Seven teacher, addressed us. On special days Mr. Hand, the headmaster, spoke; the boys marched across from the Moreton Bay fig-trees; the band came in its red and gold uniform, with the silver flutes, and the fat boy who beat the drum. We saluted the flag, and said we were Australians; that we loved our country and honoured our king and obeyed his laws. We sang 'The Song of Australia' — about the sunburned country I could not find — and 'God Save the King'. On Anzac Day and Remembrance Day we stood still for a minute that went on and on; on Arbor Day we went down the street to plant a tree.

And we read of Black Diamond the pit pony who worked in the dark and was blind when she came up to the light; I prayed that I would not be picked to read the ending because I knew I would cry. We read of Grace Darling and the wreck of the Hesperus; recited 'I Wandered Lonely as a Cloud' and 'Nicholas Nye'. We made cartridge-paper maps and charted the industries with wool and matchsticks, salt and grains of wheat. We wrote compositions, had spelling tests, and did dictation; we sang songs about the nut-brown maiden and the lass of Richmond Hill, embroidered needle-cases, drew Jonathan apples and flower-pots. I copied a picture of a lady in a crinoline saying goodbye to a soldier in a red coat, called 'The Last Adieu'. I held it up at the front because it was the best.

Then I was in Grade Six, and in September I would be eleven. All the boys had gone — there were just girls again. Mrs. Caire was our teacher. She was a fat woman, and we pretended that Mr. Goodman was her boy friend; girls were always saying they saw them kissing after school. Because I was the tallest I led the marching; I turned in the wrong direction, and Mrs. Caire told me I was stupid; I was sent to the back in disgrace. Everyone looked at me and I went red; my eyes filled with tears; the bird danced in my chest. I never led the class again.

Some girls were members of a secret society called the Caterpillar Club. They made long cloth sausages like the ones Carol's mother used to keep out the draughts; they tied them about their waists after school. They did something rude — they got into trouble. All the sausages disappeared.

In winter we ate our lunch in the shed, and bought hot pies from the Blue Shop lady who came to the gate with her trolley. Sometimes I went home to lunch, and Janice Budden and Rosemary Hearn came too; we listened to the 'Dr. Paul' serial on the wireless, and wondered what would happen next. Sometimes my grandmother made egg and bacon sandwiches and potato-chips she put into a paper cone; she handed them to me over the gate at half past twelve. The other girls were jealous; said that I was spoilt.

In winter I wore my raincoat with the pixie-hood. Chérie Russell had Wellington boots as well. We walked down the back lane together, and she poked her finger in and out of the slit in her coat and pretended she was a boy.

The berries fell from the pepper-trees; we trod them into puddles and made rainbows. The oil twisted and coiled like the patterns when we did marbling for the *Children's Hour* covers in the classroom tray.

Then it was the end of the year, and we marched across the yard for the final assembly. The band played, Mr. Hand spoke, and we all clapped. The sun was shining and I wanted a drink of water. Jennifer Toy looked down at the breasts that poked already through her dress and sniggered. I could see Ronny Morrison's head by the flagpole. Then the duxes of the two Grade Seven classes went up to get their prizes; the microphone shrieked with static, as we sang 'God Save the King'.

EIGHTEEN

WHEN I was ten years old I was given a cocker-spaniel puppy. I came home from school for lunch and he was there.

He was black and white, with curly ears that waved in and out like sooty waterfalls. He had a moist nose like a pepper-pot; eyes that were as worried and brown as Reece's. He was frightened, and slipped about the verandah on little paws. He cried for his mother and trembled in a corner.

When I came home from school in the afternoon he was still there. I realized that he was mine. I lifted him up and examined him carefully.

I saw the pink undersides of his ears, the pools of moisture that welled his eyes, the patch of prickly silver under his chin. I parted his legs and stroked the blunt stub with its feathery tuft; peered at the crêpiness beneath. I forced his jaws apart, and counted his teeth; examined his liver-coloured mouth, the sponginess of his raspberry tongue. He had a patch of whiteness on his chest and two back legs. He had a pedigree and a name: Kanarvah Laddie. I called him Tinker.

Tinker grew and became a dog.

His coat became ruffled and dishevelled; bantam-rooster feathers festooned his legs. The satin pincushions under his paws grew hard, but the little seams

114

between stayed mushroom-soft and were pierced by three-cornered jacks and rose thorns; I had to hurt him to get them out. His crinkled ears grew long and dragged in the grass—I probed for tufted thistles, and put in canker powder from the brown glass jar.

Billy, the Persian cat, disliked my dog. One day they fought, and Billy jumped on the table in the passage; froze hump-backed beside the urn. The balloon lady fell off, the table was scratched, my mother was angry. One day Billy, who was old already, became older still; pulled the hair from his coat, got thin. A man from the Council took him away—I never saw his green eyes, his tortoise-shell fur again.

Tinker was excited when I took him for a walk: ran down the passage and through the open door; I ran too, and the door slammed shut on my fingers—the second finger on my right hand was squashed and flat and hurt; the nail went blue and then purple and then black—it fell off; I saw a new one coming underneath. He got excited when I chased him up the path beside the plant that bloomed every seven years; I slipped on the gravel, and the stones were flecked with geranium petals that were blood—there was a zigzag pain, the smell of disinfectant, and my grandmother's fingers turned cruel. Afterwards they said I should have had stitches.

Tinker was my dog; I loved him dearly. I wrapped a shawl about him to a tight cocoon and sat in the gutter; held him in my arms: he was little Hiawatha, my black papoose—I told him he was better than any pink pig of a human baby. I pinned his ears to the top of his head with my fingers and he looked like Carmen Miranda. I dressed him in socks and a frock; carried him about with his paws upon my shoulders. I took him for walks on the end of a plaited leash; we sat on the seat at the tram stop and waited for my mother. I ate, and he watched with pitiful eyes until I could eat no more; I ate, and gave him the apple cores he loved—that he crunched to a milky pap. I put him in the cupboard in the bedroom and shut the door; I heard him whimpering inside and felt the same joy as when I tormented Reece; I opened the door and I was Tinker's Saviour—delivered him from the darkness, held him close.

Tinker was my dog, he was my brother. He snored in a nest of blankets, curled upon my toes all night; in the morning I found him still asleep, but draped in my petticoat, fallen to the floor. He fitted under my arm when it was dark and lit my way up the passage; shone with my mother's matches down the path at night. He was at my side when I wandered the wet garden with no shoes in winter; his satin paws and my feet turned to pumice on the same cruel stones. He comforted me when I cried, licked the tears away with his tongue; sometimes he shared my sorrow and cried too. He was particular about his food: Nan bought boneless mutton from the butcher, cooked it till it was tender on the stove.

In summer my dog's coat became matted, his ears were stuck with burrs. I took the scissors and clipped till he was cool and a little black sheep. I cut carefully round the scallops of his diminished ears until suddenly he yelped: there was blood on my fingers, and also on one sooty ear.

In summer my dog became dirty, and I washed him. Nan swathed me in a hessian apron and prepared two troughs of water. We put him in the first one; he struggled to be out, and I pushed him back and rubbed with Velvet soap. I dried him on the lawn under the fig-tree, combed his ears and brushed until I thought him dry. Then I let him go, and Nan protested that it was too soon; it was—he rolled in the ashes under the quince-tree, came back proudly, dirtier than before.

Tinker had a pink thing. He was shameless, and showed it always when there was company; dragged himself across the verandah, with it poking out like strawberry jelly—like Nan's new coral lipstick in a grey felt case. My grandmother said he had it because he was a male. She shuddered, and went away saying 'filthy beast' and 'dirty dog'.

Tinker was spoilt. He howled like a baby at the gate when we went out; we crept away with quiet voices and muffled doors to trick him, but to no avail—his awful voice echoed down the street. He found the book from the library and chewed the corners, dotted the cover with teeth; we disguised the damage in brown paper, and my mother came with me to explain; but the librarian was cross—we had to pay.

Tinker was different from other dogs, and except for walks on the leash, did not go out. He ran away when a strange dog sniffed his arse. He was soothed in my arms when it was Guy Fawkes' Night, and slumbered on while Doogles died next door.

And I think my dog with the ruffled legs and raspberry tongue, the strawberry jelly pink thing and coat thatched with leaves will never change.

He does.

Another summer comes and the lane is alive with

weeds. Out of the stony earth spring the poke-bonnets of Salvation Jane, the soft plumes of cat's ear and hare's tail, mouse-ear chickweed and vanilla-scented holy grass. The grey men from the Council come with their siphons of weed-killer. The grasses stay their fingers with ribwort and couch-grass and convolvulus; dapple their trouser legs with capeweed, the yellow pennies of shepherd's purse. Uselessly.

And somehow Tinker is there. The novelty of men and weeds is too much for him: he barks furiously with the ecstasy of it all. And, somehow, the men from the Council can kick at him with their pollen-studded boots, squirt with their chemicals in his wide brown eyes.

In an instant the Tinker who frolicked nimble-footed on the lawn, and jumped so surely onto the bed is gone. We see him coming back along the path. Slowly. He bumps into the clothes-line. And cries.

And that is how it will always be: his head held low to protect himself, his body edging sideways; his eyes vacant and milky. Blind.

NINETEEN

WHEN I found the book in the shed I began to worry about my soul. It was called *Hannah Lee, or Rest for the Weary*; was written by the author of *Isabel, or Influence, Margaret Browning, etc.*; was published by the Religious Tract Society. On the flyleaf in faded ink was written: 'Presented to Mary Davis, by the Houghton Wesleyan Sunday School, October 6th., 1876.'

Mary Davis was Aunt Poll, but this did not make me feel better.

I sat in the shed after school each day, and read from Chapter I called 'The Prayerless Home' to Chapter XXVIII called 'Rest for the Weary'. I looked at the engravings of Hannah accepting a flower, saying grace before the meagre meal, lost in the snow-storm, restored to her father. I read of the death-bed of Mrs. Owen, the aged Christian; of the miserly Miss Brownrig and the fireless hearth; of tender compassion and sweet peace the world knoweth not.

It was all very strange; I did not understand how the life I read about fitted into mine. I worried that we did not say grace at meals; that we did not go to church. I comforted myself that at least I was christened, even if it was as a Roman Catholic; that once, until a boy and

119

a bulldog chased me home, I went to the Methodist Sunday School in George Street.

But that was not enough.

I asked Nan if I could say grace before we ate; did so, in a pious voice I did not recognize. I pinned a note to my pillow reminding myself that there were prayers to be said when I awoke. I made a list of all my past ages, and tried to recall my states of grace. I felt that my life was but a dream: saw myself reclining with God on a shirred cloud watching another who lived in Rose Street perform the pantomime of school and home. I read the Catholic books that were my father's, gazed at the picture of the Virgin—but I could not understand, feared that books and pictures were tainted with popery. On Sundays I copied verses from the Bible that was my grandfather's, gazed at the lemon-drop Dianas—felt bored, thought I must be truly damned.

I was happiest with my late-nineteenth-century books. I found others as well as *Hannah* in the shed. My favourites were *The Family Friend* of 1870, and *Home Words for Heart and Hearth.* I became immersed in an Anglicized world of curtsies and village smithies, bairnies and little maids. Mention of the great wilderness that was London, waifs and strays, scanty pittances and wretched habitations could not dispel the glamour of that bygone age.

While the sun beat on the iron roof and Nan called me to collect manure in the lane, I was with those others hastening homeward through foggy streets from the *Hand and Heart* Christmas dinner. I put out crumbs for the sparrows in the snow-storm, skated with Polly and little Amy on the pond. I took the excursion train westward to dear old Wales, and climbed to the top of Snowdon. I rested under the hawthorn's shade, and watched the flowery swathes yield to the victorious scythe. I saw the bosom of the deep caress the Eddystone lighthouse; toasted muffins before the fire and heard dear pussy purring low.

I was familiar with England's martyr bishops and the martyrdom of Polycarp, with the Temperance Question and the doctrine of the Trinity, with Flora McDonald and the stately homes of England. I read pages entitled: 'The Bible Mine Searched', 'Scripture Questions', and 'Soul Food'; stories called: ' "Don't Tell!" or, The Factory Girl's Secret', 'Wise Words for the Wedded', and 'The Mother's Vow'.

I was suffused with a melancholy awareness that approximated happiness at the thought of my own and others' failings. I read a series on infidel books and urged Nan to turn from the *True Confessions* under the mattress. I talked of Satan clothing himself like an angel of light, of fatal poisoning of the soul, of discerning between the precious and the vile, and marvelled at my eloquence. My grandmother did not seem convinced; looked perplexed; decided to smile. I prayed harder than ever that she would be one with Christ.

And so when Betty Smith asked me to attend the Mile End Baptist Sunday School with her and Joan, I felt that I was one of the truly chosen. I had to walk across the Beach Road by myself, but this was as nothing to salvation. I turned up Victoria Street and met the twins under the walnut-tree beside the church. We went into the hall and I was put into Miss Enid Scott's class. I sat on a bench on the girls' side and the Sunday School superintendent talked to us. She didn't wear lipstick. We sang hymns, recited verses, and marched to our classes, where I was given a book to colour.

It was a far cry from the rarefied world of the once Bishop of Gloucester and Bristol, whom I decided looked sensitive in *Home Words*, and took as my mentor. I signed a pledge of total abstinence from alcoholic beverages; thought of tobacco as Devil's weed. I learned that a Christian did not need an insurance policy or a bank account—it was enough to believe. I told my mother this and she laughed.

There was a Sunday School Anniversary, and I sang with the others on the platform; a Harvest Thanksgiving Festival with light refreshments. There was a Missionary Evening, and a black man showed slides of camels, and Jesus' face flickered and disappeared on the back wall; a Concert, and I was a daffodil in crêpe paper.

When I went to Sunday School my hair was freshly washed, and so tightly curled that it went frizzy and my head hurt. I wore my wedgie sandals and the dress with the velvet bows upon the yoke. I had a shoulder-bag studded with silver pimples and a straw hat trimmed with rose-buds. I carried coloured pencils and a hymn book. I had a feeling deep inside I looked a fool.

I marched on my Christian way, regardless, until a Sunday came when I saw someone had written on the fence under the walnut-tree that I stank. And I knew I was different, and wished they had put 'smells'. I feared I was doomed to eternal damnation, but I would not go again.

And so I heard no more the song we crooned as we dropped our pennies in the collection box. Never again did I feel the touch of the peacock's feather the teacher stroked our heads with as we left. No more was I part of the tableau dressed as a heathen with a blackened face. The picnics at Lobethal and the fronds we were given on Palm Sunday, the egg-and-spoon races and the Harvest Festivals ceased.

Left to myself, conscience nagged.

I heard the kookaburra laugh on Sunday mornings and felt sinful at my sloth; worried that I was not up and dressing for the class. I heard the voices of the Salvation Army and was sure they had chosen our house to stand outside because I was there. When the lady in the squashed bonnet rang the bell I gave her all my pennies in exchange for a card ornamented with snowdrops and: 'Be not drunk with wine, wherein is excess; but be filled with the Spirit. —Eph. v.18' in gold underneath.

I no longer whispered with the others in Religious Instruction, but folded my arms priggishly, and listened hard; memorized the names of the figures in long robes who hovered magically on the green baize board. It was like magic as the minister created one by one on the greenness the hills and stars, the sheep and shepherds, the stable and the baby. I looked forward to the hour on Thursday before lunch, until one day someone came from the Church of Christ: it was Dean Black's father who took the Boys' Brigade. He told jokes about Catholics and did not pronounce his aitches; he made the disciples sound like a football team. The delicate world of miracles and Virgin Births I had created for myself on the shores of a Lake Galilee, that looked like the placid Windermere in the poetry book, disappeared. I felt loftily otherworldly as the class laughed at the jokes I thought were common; as Mr. Black stopped on the way out, and asked me when I would be coming to Endeavour.

I persuaded my mother to take me to church. We went to the evening service at the Methodist one the bulldog chased me from. We followed the prim backs of the two Misses Bailey from the newsagent and stationer's shop on the Beach Road.

I felt that everyone was staring as we filed in. The pews were hard, and there was a funny smell. I watched the minister's Adam's apple bob up and down. My mother was frozen under her pill-box with the little veil. We hurried out at the end, but the preacher was there first—waylaid us with his handshake. More strange people stared, and a woman with a birthmark said she hoped we would come again.

Of course we never did.

The programme on the wireless was called 'The Voice of Prophecy'. The voice that prophesied was American. Gargled with honey and treacle and golden syrup. It was beautiful—like a film star's. It quavered over the appeals, hesitated apologetically before rebukes. As I listened to the stories, cried over the sermons, and chanted the hymns I invented a father for myself. He was tall and gentle and looked like the Jesus in the Sunday School picture surrounded by the red and yellow and pink children, with a black one on His lap.

I sent away for the set of Bible Lessons, and each week I completed one and sent it in to the voice; each week it came back with ticks and comments in the margin. When I folded my question paper and licked the envelope and stuck on the stamp, I felt safe and washed clean in the blood of the Lamb. I pretended I was posting my answers to Jesus. I knew about Daniel and Moses, I could recite the names of the generations of the Children of Israel: I was a scholar.

One day in summer when I was sewing dresses for my doll, the door-bell rang. Nan went to answer it, came back very red in the face, with a funny smile; said there was a gentleman to see me. I went to the door and knew she was listening at the window.

The gentleman was stout with a dark suit and a brocade tie slashed by a pin. He was from 'The Voice of Prophecy'—it was he who had read my questions every week. But it was all wrong, for although his voice was American, it was not *the* voice; and his shoulders were so broad, his legs so thick. He was embarrassed, because he had been expecting an adult; I was embarrassed, because the Jesus image had been replaced by a real man with eyebrows that met in the middle, gold fillings in his teeth, hairs on his wrists, stiffer ones up his nose.

Once again I knew it was ruined; that I had been found out. I knew that I had cheated—I did not fit into the cosy mould I had erected so carefully. Once again the defences that guarded me from my worry had crumbled away.

I gazed at the tie-pin as he talked. I saw a black and white butterfly in a cobweb. I pushed a dead leaf under the mat with my toe. And then he shook my hand and gave me some papers from his briefcase. A signet-ring with a ruby cross sniggered, and he was gone. I went inside and threw the papers in the bin; hated my grandmother for making me see him alone. But she was unrepentant, and said that it would teach me.

It did.

I never listened to the voice again, and I ceased thinking of my Jesus father. I put *Hannah Lee* and *Home Words* and *The Family Friend* away. When Sunday came I called for Carol and we played dress-ups in the shed, had penny concerts, turned cartwheels on the lawn.

But I came to hate Sunday. The cartwheels and the concerts could not dispel the awful feeling inside me when I heard the church bells ring.

TWENTY

I STARED at the baby. Its skin was uniformly cream, there were no flushes on its cheeks—just a nose, the creases of eyes, a curved mouth. The baby looked as if it had been carved from soap or stitched in padded velvet. Then the creases opened and the creaminess was blemished by ugly smudges.

The baby was the brother of the girl who stole my oranges. I stood in her mother's kitchen and smelt talcum powder and milk and napkins. I forgot the baby and felt miserable as I remembered Gymnasium. I counted the days that remained until I went again. I added the nights to make the time longer.

I did not choose to go to Gymnasium (shoulders that droop, a chance remark of the girl who steals my oranges—they send me there). I felt cold and strangely tall (my Italian-cloth shorts cling to my thighs, my ankles are branded by blancoed sandshoes) as I walked down Rose Street each Friday evening.

I did not have far to walk, for the class was held in the room above the Sno-Whyte Bag Laundry. (As I take off my coat I gaze at the lights of the houses below. I cross the room and look at the stiff moon that hangs in the tree by the gate.)

I did not know why I hated going.

Perhaps it was the smell of my sandshoes. It may

have been the way the medicine balls flew through the dusty air (my body is pale and vulnerable, my arms are weak—I cannot throw the basketball). Perhaps it was the ever-changing instructress with the nagging whistle, who, because ever changing, was seen as someone blurred and indefinite, confused in similarities with her predecessor: the same legs knotted at the thigh with muscle, blossoming at the calf with a bruise; the same angry clasp of bloomers round secret flesh; the same prim neckline that revealed abundance when she did the abdominal squeeze.

I did not know why I kept on going.

At first I was afraid to stop because of the girl who stole my oranges—but then she moved away. At first I went because it pleased my mother and my grandmother—and besides, it was so near. But the class moved too: from the room above the laundry to a hall next to the Methodist Church where I did not find God.

And still I did not leave.

(I linger to watch the Seniors arrive. They come as we put on our coats. The big girls wear short frocks, and I wonder at their legs; watch an assortment of gold chains and hearts and little crosses bob as breasts and a shadow in-between jump up and down. The boys alarm me with their hairiness—some silky like monkeys, others ginger and curly like cats. I come closer, and see pin-pricks under the girls' arms; more hairs under the boys'.)

We did trunk twists, alternate toe touching, and side bends. We danced to the music of a piano, caught bean-bags that shivered, swung Indian clubs. There was a wooden horse with a padded top I hated; marching practice that I liked, until someone said I pointed my toes and looked funny.

(I lie on the floor and look up the leg of the girl in front. I see bright red at the crotch. And as I watch the leg rises higher, the redness grows bigger—becomes an avid mouth. I wonder what is wrong.)

There was a camp in the hills at Mount Lofty. I had never been away from home; my mother said it would do me good.

Nan waved me off at Victoria Square beside the statue of Sturt peering through his telescope. The bus looked the same as the one that took us to Houghton; it was I who made it different: I felt peculiar and alone, although I was surrounded by all the others. Then we waved, and Nan's face and blue hair grew paler; faded completely. I felt the same as I did when I was seven and my mother went on the Gulf Trip. I pressed my nails into my hand so I wouldn't cry.

I could not concentrate on the trees and the gardens and the winding road; I was conscious of the others about me. They were all older. There were the Hood twins and their big sister Phyllis who went to the High School. There was Yvonne Heath whose father died in the War; she was beautiful with dimples and sausage curls her mother put up in rag curlers; she could tap-dance, do the Highland fling in a Scottie's kilt. There were girls whose names I did not know.

Everyone stopped talking and gasped as we went round the Devil's Elbow; pointed at the stuffed bird on top of the Eagle on the Hill Hotel. When we got to Mount Lofty it began to rain; we walked to the hostel with our cases, and there was cocoa to drink that was too sweet. The seam between the legs of my pants bothered me and made it hard to walk; I wished I knew where the lavatory was. When I found it I saw a rude drawing and finger-marks and wished I had not come. We made our beds and I felt left out as the other girls saved places for their friends, and whispered in a corner.

I went for a walk by myself. I found an empty box, and decided to fill it with beautiful things. I carpeted it with moss, and it looked like my mother's jewel-case with the watered-silk lining. My jewels were toadstools, an empty snail-shell, ivy leaves that looked like stars, pebbles that were cool against my cheek, some wattle, gum leaves with holes, a feather. My jewel-case became a garden; I found a piece of glass, embedded it in the moss—it was a castle; I put the feather behind—it was a fountain.

When I showed my garden to the others, Yvonne Heath said it was pretty and Phyllis Hood said it was nice. But someone giggled.

There was a storm in the night, and the lights of Adelaide wriggled below us; the sky was cut by lightning. In the morning when I went to get my box I found it had been kicked—the mossy garden was crumpled, the fountain bent, the castle broken. My garden was no more. The others said it was sad.

(We go for a hike, and pass houses with rhododendron drives and columns. I see pears hanging to ripen from the rafters of a verandah, foxgloves, a notice that says: PLUMS TOMS KIDNEY BEANS VICTORIAS FOR SALE. We pass trees full of apples, black and white cows, sunshades fallen on the lawns of a hotel. I see sheets hung to dry amongst dahlias, trees that look like umbrellas . . . We cook our food over a fire and buy black currant éclairs at a shop. I think we must have walked miles, and my sock keeps slipping under my heel. I go behind a bush to wee; get stung by nettles — do it on my shoe. It begins to rain again, and we get soaked. I am conscious of how dirty we look, of our mud-stained shoes, our unruly hair, the way people in cars stare as they pass . . . We walk back through the hills that are wet and dark; all the time I miss my mother and grandmother, Tinker and Reece . . . I feel hurt by the talk and laughter of the others; the way they tramp uncaring through the grass — ignoring the orchids, the curly rims of the geraniums, the sweet-scented fluff of the thorn . . . My face feels strained from trying to smile — it is a mummy-face wrapped in gauze. My smile grows stiffer; at last it disappears . . . I plod on; comfort myself by remembering that tomorrow I will be home . . . Yet even as I do, I wonder why it should be that once I leave the Rose Street world, I am no longer me.)

The day passed, and another night; we went back to the city, and my grandmother looked different after two days' absence. At the end of the year I was presented with an Enid Blyton book as the most improved Junior.

When the new year came I remembered my box (toadstools, an empty snail-shell, ivy leaves that looked like stars, pebbles that were cool against my cheek, some wattle, gum leaves with holes, a feather) and did not go again.

TWENTY-ONE

Mrs. Newton, at the end of Rose Street, was important for a summer. She had a mulberry-tree in her garden; Carol and I had silkworms. Each day after school we lifted the latch on the gate, followed the winding path to the tree, climbed its twisted branches. Mrs. Newton was a widow; she cried when she thought of her husband. We saw her, through the heart-shaped leaves, weeping like a little wise monkey; stick-fingers shielding her eyes.

We came home with the leaves and exchanged them for old ones nibbled away. There was the smell of savoury greenness; our fingers parried gently with pale silkworm flesh. One day we found our worms become crooked shadows—brides in veils of silk. Then the cones grew opaque; we stopped gathering leaves. Mrs. Newton and her tears were forgotten.

I was anxious to see what would happen next, but I had to forfeit my box. I was going away for my first holiday with my grandmother, my mother, and Reece.

We were going past the trees at the end of the street, the parklands and spires of the city; past Glenelg and the gum-tree, the Cove Roads and Ocean Boulevards of Marino, to Port Noarlunga.

Tinker was sent to a dogs' home, and my cardboard

132

box was put on the roof. I left the lid off so the moths could fly away.

We waited at the bus station with our cases, and I heard a wireless play a song about a little organ-grinder with a monkey on a stick. And the chorus mocked saucily: 'Oh mumma-mia, a monkey on a stick.'

We drove past the almond orchards of Marion and crossed the Sturt River, climbed O'Halloran Hill and saw the Happy Valley reservoir. We passed the churches and vineyards of Reynella and a house with an iron roof that hurt my eyes and candle pines cut into roosters and peacocks. Then I saw sand-hills, and the loops of the Onkaparinga River, and blueness that stretched for ever.

We got off and walked up the hill and there were bushes spotted with strange red insects and a house called Western Glen. We had three rooms on the first floor. We shared a bathroom with the other guests, and my mother told me not to stand on the wooden mat as I might get foot disease.

Soon the days exactly the same dissolved into one long day.

We walk down the steps and round the side, past the entwined bushes of old man and old woman. We carry a beach-umbrella and a rug, raffia baskets and towels, a rubber ball and a thermos. The sun falls boldly on my city body; I am aware of my white skin, the thinness of my legs, the veins that nestle inside my elbows. Nan's linen bodice swings rhythmically under its rows of pin-tucks and pearly buttons. Reece clasps her hand and trots stiffly, wearing her public expression and print frock, her face an ugly shade of plum, her eyes sulky under the brim of her hat. My mother disengages herself, and lags a pace or two behind, the Kodak camera round her neck.

We walk along the road past the boarding-houses and the chalky cliffs laced with grass. Below us is the sea. Above our heads gulls circle ceaselessly; shiny bull-ants scamper at our feet. We climb jerkily down the slope, past the crooked pines and the shelter shed where yesterday my mother and I read *True Confessions* in the rain. We take our shoes off, for we have reached the sand, and I am conscious that the man lying on his stomach with the peeled skin map on his back has turned his head to look at Reece.

I am glad when we round the corner and come to the first cave. And pass it; erect the beach-umbrella.

Nan and Reece and my mother rest while I clamber the shallow steps of a limestone terrace. I have a secret place here: a gritty throne beside a twisted thorn-bush that shades me from the sun. I search in the limestone crevices for buried treasure, but find only lolly papers and a fretwork of initials. I creep up the hump of a rock, and eavesdrop, hearing voices. I determine to find lovers, like those I saw under the willows, but am disappointed—it is only a family party the same as ours.

And if, in the long summer days that are all alike, we do not stab our beach-umbrella into the sand near my limestone throne, we go further afield to the sand-dunes.

They are in the other direction: away from the caves and the sun-bathers; past the jetty. Here.

Here, in the haunt of seagulls with red bills and redder

feet, we camp. My mother unsheathes the Kodak Brownie, and immortalizes us all with her finger.

(We were still there twenty years later: Reece, sitting like an Egyptian statue on a rock, toes turned in — massive. My grandmother, sprawled careless on the sand, her silver hair curling, her red lips smiling, a handkerchief in her hand. I, amongst sea-rocket and spinifex, in a dress that is too short; kneeling like St. Francis in a fairy-ring of blurred specks that are birds.)

Here grows the she-oak, the pandanus, and the tea-tree. I find little low creeping things as in the hills: variable groundsel, small-leaved clematis, magenta noon-flower that Nan calls pig's-face. There are sand-flowers and tissue-paper sea-violets, cat's ears and pussy tails that I take home to paint — and forget. There are sand-hoppers that whirr, bleached cuttlebones and bread-crumb sponge, bird skeletons, fish bones, and everywhere the mumble of the sea.

The sea is so big.

Sometimes I turn from its vastness and seek a space of my own. I creep over the low rocks. I am an Indian; I am a tiger. In and out of shadow and light I creep, sunburned and dappled. Over a honeycomb of rocks that look like islands of bone.

Far away is the steely sea I shun, falling in stripes on the sand. Before me is the world I seek.

I am the Indian; I am the tiger. I am Gulliver.

I peer through the clefted melon of my bottom, through the looped curtains of my feet, and into the rock pool swims a face.

I see a moving forest of sea-lettuce and wrack; a garden where sea-anemones quiver in a bower of eelgrass, and something pinkish and soft caresses a sludge-brown mussel. Little stones hurtle stilly: blue-grey and mottled, terracotta and creamy-orange — incised with lines, pock-marked with scabs and iridescent sparkle, smooth as silk, crested with barnacles. And even as I look, a stone betrays me — the water ripples, a crab scuttles away.

There are days when it is wet, and I play heedless in the shallows; wander in a sea mist; sit in the shelter shed and pretend to sight mermaids. There are days when it is warm, and I bury myself in the cool sand; pose for a photograph in a seaweed boa; chase the shadow of the jutting cliff.

(And slowly the shadow crept over the beach. The sea unfurled itself like a length of silk; waves seamed and met in pleats that shirred to nothing. The dunes turned blue; the tawny patchwork fell from the rocks; the sun was a lemon, a slice of Jaffa orange, a golden hump, a wink — and was gone. Red insects were blotted, caves washed clean of sea-shell garlands. The night cut new initials on my limestone throne; strangers cradled the thorn-bush.)

When the morning comes I cannot find my rock pool, my mermaid, my seaweed boa. My white skin turns raw and freckled; the map I saw on others' backs appears on mine.

(My first holiday was almost over.)

We go for a walk down a green lane — Nan and Reece, my mother and I (and dust hung over the grass, the pine-trees were ripped by wind, the lovely lady had sunburned arms). We come out by tennis-courts, and watch figures behind wire-netting leap for a ball that taunts them with 'ping'. Then my mother and I buy our tickets at the depot—already I am late for school. Nan and Reece wave us away and I am sad.

When we dropped from the vineyards and the orchards to the sameness of the suburbs it was dark.

I held my mother's hand. We walked from the tram stop with the suitcase that bumped my leg. I had my mother's scarf on, patterned with masks and ribbons. It smelt of her body and her perfume and the single cigarette she smoked at night.

We clasped chips we bought from the Greek and followed the paw marks, frozen deep in the concrete, of a dog that was not there. They went past the hoardings by the side of Hook's, and the wooden fence that said AMGOORIE, and stopped at the lane I feared. I thought I saw a white tail wag, and was scared as we scurried across the black gulf and into the light again.

The key would not open the door. My mother got in at the window like a robber. I felt more afraid than ever as I waited on the gravel. The roses were so pale, the lilies gleamed, the gravel hissed.

The house was fusty from being shut up; milk smelt in a saucepan we forgot. We ate the chips without a cloth. Already I missed my grandmother. It was strange to be there with my mother—the two of us alone.

My mother came with me to the Primary School. I was late, and we saw the deputy headmaster, who looked like Humphrey Bogart, and he smiled at my mother and told her it didn't matter. And I felt proud, for I wore my mother's scarf, and the other girls would know I had been on holiday.

THE SCENT OF EUCALYPTUS

The next day Tinker came back from the dogs' home. He is thin and has fleas and his turds are white.

The next day I climbed the ladder to the roof and my box. And I only see ants; and the frail bodies of moths—their wings all eaten away, trying to rise from the silky cages that bind them.

At the end of the week Nan and Reece came back from the sea.

TWENTY-TWO

Miss Monk the Grade Seven teacher is funny looking—face like a walnut or a peach stone, hair in a bun all crinkly and it falls out and goes round her face like cobwebs. She looks almost like a witch, although it's not a nice thing to say—but the little hairs are like the down on a nettle (all along her lip) and even a moustache as well and false teeth and orange gums that aren't real and crooked body. She also looks something like the lady on the ship, but with her clothes on, and when she runs for the basketball her front goes up-and-down, but you never see anything because she can't bend over—too stiff. And her legs—thick stockings, not quite lisle and funny dresses—long, nearly to her ankles (one with daisy-chains and one just plain) and buttons and a pin like a clover and a wrist watch but not very fancy—not diamanté, and hat like a Scottie's.

Miss Monk stepped stiffly from the tram clasping her worn black handbag and the leatherette school-case that contained the exercise books she had marked the night before. (And all those little ticks and crosses made me miss Lux Playhouse, and no Milo even, before I went to bed—but then, after all, I am the Lady Deputy, and take the basketball—not bad for a lass from Berri, even if I say it. But sometimes I even think of Berri and all the oranges and the river even and wish I were back. For

Holy Trinity Methodist by the lilac and the Variety Concert by the scholars that was very nice, and also Rev. Blackett. But not now—it was actually quite some time ago and I haven't been back since, nor eaten the oranges. They are still there though—not too many pips, not too thick a skin.) And her sponge-bag (plastic with a draw-string and Pear's soap worn down very thin and a flannel that's a bit dirty but I've my white towel in the drawer, and lavender on my hanky—that's all—no lipsticks or eye-stuff for me—anyway, too old— mutton dressed as lamb), and her lunch in brown paper (egg sandwich and queen cakes and an apple, tea provided by the school—and don't we need it), and a handkerchief (hem-stitch border with E.M. and the lavender). She walked down the Beach Road and in at the gate (lolly papers about), in at the door—into the classroom. She hung her coat on a peg behind the door, examined her face in the mirror, hurried into the yard as the bell rang, and blew her whistle.

And we hear the bell and have to stop skippy and Miss Monk comes and blows the whistle and hurry, because she hits. She has a stick and fall in and left–right into school and you try and see the boys, but too far. And through the cloakroom and past old Goodman's room (Mrs. Caire is his girl friend) and then into the room and it's big and all khaki, with desks the colour of toffee, but scratched all over with names and initials you can't quite see. Mine has a flag on it too, and a big- nose face, and a map of Australia that didn't come out right, and lots of ink blots. And when we get in we stand up straight and say Good Morning, Miss Monk, and she answers and we all sit down, then calls the roll and we say Present, Miss Monk. And out the window is the Beach Road and you can hear the cars and the trams very loud, even though there is a garden, but the things don't grow very well, and see the men from the second-hand shop and the lady from the Blue Shop coming with her trolley and the pasties for the Tech girls (that means it's nearly recess) and up further Vanity Fayre Hair Beauty, where they burnt my mother's hair. I sit by the window so I see it all, but once I ate a stickjaw and she asked me to read and I had it in my mouth—found me out, and now hold out your hand.

And if it was February there were the interminable lists of books.

We have the book lists and trips to the Book Room and come to school with florins in a green pound note or in your hanky or even in a tin. And can watch the ones who are poor and cannot afford it and they get called out and into trouble. What a shame. I love the chalky smell of the new books—blank books are red the colour of rust and line books blue and dear little memo and drawing book (I'm the best) and pastel book like fur with tissue-paper in between but I don't like the arithmetic or the geography. I like the reader and the history.

And if it was February, Miss Monk, as graciously as that other virgin ruler ever did, dispensed her patronage —created her monitors. There were monitors for flowers and tea and ink and books and blackboard and library and fire and windows.

The tea monitors are the ones I'd like to be—then you can get away from geography before lunch and after-noon assembly when we had to stand there in the sun and a girl even fainted. I got all sunburned and Nan had to rub in Calamine—it was all we'd got, even if it's really for hives. And the tea monitors can fill the urn and put out the cups and go down to Keogh's for the biscuits and not pay and put their fingers in the hot water when it's cold and talk to Miss Roebuck who is very pretty and has ankle-straps and dirndl skirts. I wouldn't mind being an ink monitor though, but you dirty your hands, but you can boss and there's the ink bottle with the spout like a cocky's beak and you give out nibs as well. Collect the inkwells like top hats on Friday and wash them out and the troughs all go blue and they clink. You get your hands dirty, but I like the smell—as good as Velvet soap or Lion coffee essence. The blackboard one has a felt duster and gets rid of the awful arithmetic and puts up the date with flowers at the side 3.8.51 today—nearly my birthday (next month). And flower monitors (and I was one with Miss White—she was lovely—I wrote her a letter and was her pet but she's fatter now) get all the best flowers from the bin—come in with wet leaves on their arms— they get carnations and snapdragons and sweet peas Patty Briggs always brings. Maybe better than even doing the tea. And book monitors get the homework and library ones do the books and Lorna Jones says they're always put back too tight (she is bossy) and window monitor keeps out the sun and fire monitor does the kindling and mallee roots and Leigh Creek coal and can sit in front and go out with the tongs. She keeps warm in winter. It's cold right up the back.

Miss Monk taught with a little stick in a cream and grey and treacle-coloured room with carved desks and Landseer prints and wilting pickle-jar posies. The room was scented with chalk dust and pencil shavings and mucus.

She teaches us geography and history and hit Hannibal's journey with the stick and English and I wrote the best composition about my life and had to read it out and Miss Monk said was it true. And she says we write like barbarians so we do pothooks and learn to do proper handwriting. No ball-points allowed, but some have fountain pens (not me). We get nibs from the box and Janice Budden likes the old ones best so we swop and wear them in with spit. We do general knowledge quizzes and I got mixed up with Mr. Chifley and Mr. Churchill and Friday is good because school's nearly over. And pastels and you get your fingers dirty and can't rub out and draw all-overs and borders and apples and a star with the compass, but free choice is best—I cannot do the larkspur or the poppy and got smacked to get it right.

There were tobacco-tins full of general knowledge questions for quizzes (and once I went to U.K. on the boat—some time ago now and to dear old Scotland where I got the heather and it is still in the frame, but wilted, and saw Buckingham Palace—what a beautiful sight, and Queen Mary in her toque and that other one I won't mention and the little princesses, wrong, Silly Billy—Margaret Rose wasn't even on the way, and the Tower and the Jewels and even Paris by night but not my cup of tea. And then Cornish cream teas and the cliffs all out in gorse that smelt like coconut toffee and little donkeys—quite quaint—and then back again and I said I shall never forget it. But no place like home—that was Berri then. Well I did my dash, and not done it since), and on Friday afternoons when the inkwells and vases had been emptied the room was alive with a low murmuring as if from drowsy bees.

And I read a book about the Solar System that is magic and the deputy headmaster who looks like Humphrey Bogart came in and farted by mistake (dirty pig) and we got the giggles — but under the desk. And we have autograph books — Eggs and bacon you're mistaken is a good one — last one at the back, always down the corner, or Roses are red or In my chain-of-friendship or If all the boys lived over the sea. And we do singing and Miss Monk let us do one of the wireless ones — Mocking-bird Hill. And did I.Q. tests and one day we saw in the *Advertiser* that old Goodman did adultery — and it was Mrs. Caire — she was his girl friend and Lorna Jones saw them kissing after school (hubba-hubba) and we all sat and whispered in the cloak-room when they came in. And he got sent to somewhere in the Bush but she stayed.

TWENTY-THREE

Every Tuesday, at ten minutes to seven in the morning, I had a piano lesson.

In winter, smoke came out of people's mouths. Shapes loomed fuzzily; first birds had not sung; lights still glowed along the street. Nan walked with me down the path, clutching her old grey coat; grains of sleep in her eyes, stockings full of ladders. Sometimes the rain fell on our umbrella, and the clothes-line was a string of pearls; sometimes we walked in a mist that hid the wood-yard. But always—through the rain, behind the mist—was the blueness (sometimes nearly black).

In spring it was different (. . . and escape to the sleeping garden. And so still, just the chat of birds and the air breathing quiet; then tizzies and trills and a white sky flushed with blue. It could be the Garden of Eden, but made little: no animals but Tinker—he is blind, and perhaps a mouse, and rats—for there are rats in the ivy; but mainly birds and lots of insects and pink earthworm whom I like. And daffodils yellow gone green in the hollows and jonquils milky cream, and a basin of pink that is arabis. And tassels of greenness on trees down the lane and the bamboo shoots all new), and I heard the drip-drip of the tap by the red and white geranium, tied about with grubby rag. And a quiver, just a quiver of warmth was (. . . and slowly the soot that is in the greenness is sucked out—plucked from the crinkles of the daffodils, the creamy petals of the jonquils; all the inkiness goes and everything comes clean. And there are green umbrellas and spears and stars all about the garden that will next month toss up daisies and bells that loop and sky-blue larkspurs) in the air, and as I went out the gate covered in lavatory-creeper the sun came up over the Queen of Angels'—I saw it in the distance (. . . and last month's dead leaves on the path).

It was a quarter to seven. There were men with kit-bags on bicycles, and at the end of Dew Street the milk-man and his horse. Dog excreta blossomed from the pavement.

The brushwood fence of the house was sodden with rain. The cast-iron Scotch thistle welcomed me. I pushed open the gate.

I turned the bell I could not hear ring, and sat to wait on the seat (I wonder if she heard—for once I didn't ring long enough, and she didn't hear, and I got into trouble). I had almost decided to ring again, when the glass door flushed; was opened by my teacher.

(My teacher is tall, with two brown plaits. Sometimes when I am early she is still doing them up, with a pin between her teeth. She is pale, with brown eyes. Her voice comes out like her music—little, then suddenly loud. Her nostrils quiver when she talks; she cranes her neck—it is a milky neck with twin moles. She does not wear lipstick. Her paleness is lovely; with just the eyes and the moles and the crown of hair. My teacher is romantic: she wears an engagement-ring, but Nan said her fiancé got killed in the War. Violet should be her name—like satin ribbons and bunches of grapes—but it is Dorothy.)

The music room was warm from the electric fire, and there was the smell of polish from the two pianos. I was aware of their glow, and my teacher's hands with their nails filed short, and the smell of scented soap. There were velvet chairs and lattice-paned doors. The keys of the piano had a sharp smell, as if they were washed in lemon. On top of the piano stood a metronome, a crystal vase with hyacinths, someone's photo.

First my teacher inspected my nails (for they must not be too long and echo the notes). Then she warmed my fingers, making them come alive with her hands and the sparkling ring. I felt the lovely dizziness I felt when Aunt Poll pulled up my sock by the agapanthus (I never forget). It was the same when my teacher slid beside me on the seat, and I worried my elbow would bump her chest.

(She sits so close as she writes in the fingering, and her arms are so pale. I wonder if she has dark hairs under them. I look in her eye and see a black-currant pupil swim in creamy jelly; she blinks. She sits so close. Her soft body is pressed against me. Her legs gleam under the keyboard. Her fingers with the pink nails and the diamond grasp a pencil with a gold top and a little tassel; she writes in the fingering.)

Her voice kept time with her fingers; she sang as she played. The warm room, with its faint sweet smell, shut out the morning; the crystal vase tinkled, and the hyacinths bobbed up and down. My teacher played on.

Then it was my turn (and as I play she sips a glass of water with lemon slices like yellow fish. She peels an apple and its skin falls in coils; there is greenish flesh. Her pale hands cut away the core. A bead of spit shows at her mouth). I played, and my notes sliced the lovely vagueness of the apple and its frilled skin and the silent metronome and the clock that ticked the time. And I played from *A Garden of Melodies* and *Puck's Pieces* and she said it was quite good (but my scales are very bad and also arpeggios. I have exercise books in rose-bud wall-paper and do Theory, and learn Italian words and there is curly treble like a Persian and bass clef is a fish, middle C has a bowler hat, sharps are cross-patches, notes are tadpoles. I know 'Every Good Boy Deserves Fruit' and 'FACE').

At ten minutes to eight the bell rang, and my teacher wrote in one of the exercise books the pieces I must practise for next week. I was jealous of the girl who sat on the seat.

I walked home the front way, relishing the freshness — the feeling that anything might happen. The gravel crunched underfoot; I was cut by thorns as I fished the newspaper from its rose bush cage. Nan let me in. There was the smell of sausage; I heard eggs spitting in the pan. My mother ran past in her petticoat.

At first I paid Carol's mother ten shillings a week to practise at the German piano on the verandah (but there were the cats, and Carol's mother, and then Carol got jealous and always wanted to play Chopsticks).

Then I took my ten shillings to Mrs. Scuse who was my grandmother's friend (cocky-face, dropsy husband, a piano). Mrs. Scuse lived very near Great-grandfather Collins so I had to walk down Dew Street with my head strangely averted. I was ushered into a front room with family photographs, a plastic pineapple for ice, and brass pyramids and camels and genie lamp. The piano had a hang-down music-rack and candle-brackets. An artificial coal fire spiralled; there was a clock on top of the piano that timed my hour (I have a rest at half past and watch the people coming home from work—or look into the drawers, but mustn't make a noise. And once I stopped too long and she nearly caught me).

Then one day I came home to find a piano in the sitting-room (Nan got out her old pieces and tried 'A Dream of Paradise' but said she couldn't do it—her fingers were too stiff).

I was given a music satchel for my birthday (black and a zipp and initials). I thought I was meant to be a musical genius (like the one—Cornel Wilde, I think, who went away with the long hair and lace shirt and little bag full of the earth of his land). My grandmother wished I would play something pretty (Adelaide College of Music with all the vamping).

At the end of the term there was a recital at my music teacher's house. I was not nervous. I rolled on the lawn with Tinker before I went; I did not change my dress (Nan didn't see); I wore my sandshoes (no socks). I went up the path and rang the bell. And my teacher opened it and it was dreadful for (I went all red and they all looked) everyone wore their best (smocked frocks and even a velvet and bunny-wool and suits with creases —the boys, and flash school uniforms) clothes, and there were girls from Methodist Ladies' College (maroon— M.L.C. in white), and Walford House (funny hats— grey), and Presbyterian Girls' College (P.G.C.—Scottie's uniform but green—pompon on the beret), and boys from Prince Alfred College (Princes'—ministers' sons go there—maroon pimple caps), and even St. Peter's College (Saints'—very flash—rich people go there—blue pimple caps).

I feel I am an interloper amongst this privileged coterie. The very braces they wear on their teeth, their eczema, their blackheads, their spectacles seem signs of a virtue I do not possess. I long for their fawn gloves and lisle stockings and embroidered pockets and felt hats and enamelled badges (but they're snobs—they have hyphens and don't speak; but the schools are run by ministers—Methodist and C. of E. and the other ones, so they must be better than me—the ministers must care more about them—maybe even Jesus. Lucky pigs).

At the end of the year there is a recital in the Holder Memorial Methodist Church hall. This time I wear my best clothes.

TWENTY-FOUR

WE SAT under the pepper-trees and the tree with scalloped flowers at recess talking about how you had babies, and something called menstruation. I did not think either of these things had anything to do with me, but still I felt afraid.

We watched in class for girls who had to go home suddenly, and nodded our heads; I remembered the girl at Gymnasium and the mouth under her leg. There was a girl from Hungary, whose name we could not pronounce, and it happened to her; her mother would not let her play in the basketball match, and the team lost for the first time.

Miss Monk was the basketball coach, and umpired all the games. We laughed at her as she ran backwards in her long dresses on stiff legs, blowing her silver whistle. I longed to be picked for the team—to wear the blue tunic with gold bands around the hem, to suck oranges at half-time. I saw myself at centre, but only the smallest girls were picked for that; or as the goalie, but I could not get the ball through the hoop. Because I was tall I was always chosen to be defence, and somehow my arm was not strong enough—I could not throw the ball. I was put there when Miss Monk picked the B team to play at Mount Barker, and Miss Monk blew her whistle and sent me off. I ran as fast as I could to the lavatories and locked myself in at the end and couldn't stop crying. I came out with a blotched face, and everyone looked. (And I remember for ever the spiked fence about the lavatory and the bitter prickles on the thorn-bush at one end.)

I was given pennies to spend on chocolate frogs and liquorice straps at lunch-time, and one day as I was walking back from the Daisy Dell Milk Bar I was swept suddenly with the same longing I felt at the Kindergarten, that made me run to seek my mother. The same bird with ruffled feathers fluttered in my chest, the same stones choked my throat, the same needles pricked my eyes. For my grandmother.

I ran all the way home. I crept in without her hearing, and it was funny to watch Nan and Reece without them knowing. They ate their scraps of cold roast beef left from Sunday's joint, and Nan scooped up the puddle of tomato sauce with her bread, and rested her leg that ached in Reece's lap. And Reece's belly rattled and she did not care, for she thought I couldn't hear. And I saw the little lines on Nan's face, and the red verandah was so cold and the roses were all dead.

(It is a foreboding of a time when my grandmother will be gone, and the Rose Street life will be swept away. It is a foreboding of a time when I will dream always of finding my way back to the house with the pebble-dash and the red verandah, where a bread tin stands always in readiness by a front door that does not open, for a baker who does not come. And pink roses climb for eternity up a pebble-dash wall, and cast their petals onto tinsel cinerarias and icy gravel down below.)

It was 1951. I was in Grade Seven; I was twelve years old. I was sitting for my Progress Certificate, and posed for the photograph with all the others in the boys' playground under the varnished leaves of the Moreton Bay figs. The smallest girls sat in front on a rug: Janice Rugey, next to Catherine Oates, who held her handkerchief like a water-lily; Chérie Russell, who boasted of her name that was French; Yvonne Turley, who was white-haired and eye-lashed like an albino; the Twinnies; Beverley King, the dentist's daughter, who wore a Scottie-dog pinned to her cardigan.

And behind the smallest girls we ascended miraculously into the air. I stood second from the left, in the third row from the back. My eyes were narrowed against the sun (they have disappeared to black slits). I wore the orange corduroy jacket that was my mother's over the red and blue jumper knitted in brick-pattern (but in the photograph I am dressed in black and white and grey).

And I look at the photograph twenty years later, and the black and white and grey takes on colour. I see the dark green leaves of the fig-trees, Shirley Miller's pink jumper with the brown horses' heads knitted into the front, Patty Briggs' ginger hair above lace-collared velveteen. I see Irene Carapetis' chestnut plaits and smell garlic and hear her boast of Prince Philip being Greek; I see Loris Jenning's red flannel petticoat, and remember when Roberta Starr and I were cruel, and counted the days she wore it.

And I look harder, and in between our fresh pinkness I see the faces of the girls who are poor and cannot pay for their books. They are girls who know they are different, and have no hope; girls with perpetual colds and running noses, who wear sandshoes in all weathers; girls who bring their tomato sauce sandwiches wrapped in newspaper, whose clothes are worn by others before them, or bought too big to make them last. They come from the back streets of Thebarton that smell of gas; the narrow streets by the Wheatsheaf pub, where I walked with my grandfather.

There is one of them who is beautiful and bold called Valda. She pushes her uncle along in a wheelchair; he has a disease, and is withered like a skeleton. She pushes him along, and she whispers of the things he does to her, and the things the boys do too. And even though she has her boldness and her beauty, and it is Australia and 1951, she doesn't have a chance.

(But then the photograph was new, and in black and white and grey. And, although I didn't know it, I would never see some of its faces again. Some girls were going to the High School, where they would learn Latin and French. One was going to Methodist Ladies'; Miss Monk said she ought to be glad. The rest of us went across to the Technical School, and were shown the Art Room with its water-colour cabbages, the Science Room with its bunsen burners, the Dressmaking Room with its swollen-breasted dummies. And we all sat for our Progress Certificates, and I came second. On the last day, at the last assembly I would ever stand at, after the flutes screamed madly and the fat boy beat the drum, I went out to get my prizes. I was given a certificate which entitled me to one year's free subscription to the library by the Daisy Dell. I was given a book called *Hope's Last Chance*, about a girl who played hockey, and wore fawn gloves and lisle stockings and embroidered pockets and felt hats and enamelled badges. Something like at the Tech School.)

TWENTY-FIVE

As I GREW older it was easy to forget the quiet, calm place I came from. I became accustomed to a world that others said was real.

I learn my lesson well and always wipe my feet, do the homework fast and after there is skippy and hidey and chewie and hoppy and mummy but no daddy (relax, little girl—you are almost safe), and copy down the things that pink-cheek Reverend says and Bible read and pray upon the seat; sing O Rock of Ages, hide Thou me! and listen to Rev. Voight and send in a donation very anonymous. Isn't that enough? (Not far, not far from the Kingdom, Yet in the shadow of sin; How many are coming and going!—How few there are entering in! How few there are entering in! How few there are entering in! How many are coming and going!—How few there are entering in!)

I was seduced by the smooth voices of radio announcers, the banality of soap powder jingles, the empty glamour of film-star buccaneers. I paid homage without question to a sovereign and a flag and a sunburned land that were not mine. I believed that God overlooked Adelaide as surely as Colonel Light; that he was one with the castrated angel, the apricot cathedral, the Queen and the bronze explorers, the gentleman on the horse, the marble Greeks.

I told my every thought and action to my mother in
the lavatory at night. I treasured the merit card with
its swallow and headmaster's initialled sprig. I observed
the Sabbath and read my Bible and gave pennies in buff
envelopes to missionaries in a field. I did not steal or lie
or swear — I was pure of heart and virtuous and a prig.

I emulated my mother and gloated over the Social
Pages of the *Advertiser* (page twenty-six is best). I conjured up a fabulous company of doctors' wives in electric-
blue Thai silk and lady-mayoresses swathed in Arctic
fox (Beaumont/Toorak/Burnside/Tusmore). I read ele-
vating accounts of elder sons (Alistair) that proceeded
from the cloisters of St. Peter's College *via* the Young
Liberals (who are not liberal), and the English Speaking
Union (E.S.U.), the golf-linked swards of Kooyonga
and a junior-partnership in the firm of another (Old
Blue), to the dizzy (Elysian) heights of the Adelaide
Club. I saw pictures (admittedly a little out of focus)
of younger daughters (Annabel) on their days of glory:
in tulle with pretty rose-bud posies, making pretty
curtsies from the ranks of those others from (Wood-
lands, Wilderness, all the rest) select (expensive)
private schools; in magnolia silk at Marquee Receptions
after Cathedral Weddings with other people's elder sons
(Alistair); in gardenia linen at Cathedral Christenings
of dear little babies (Alistair, Annabel) in feather-stitch
and tight French knots.

I was a stranger to this world. I could produce no requisite pedigree of ancient antipodean families seconded
from more ancient Anglican shores; no mother who
ministered at Red Cross Fêtes and hospital Spring Fairs;
no old collegiate father; no money; no brown serge

school-days—all the proofs of kinship to the world on page twenty-six. Therefore I was no one.

Yet still I was not free.

There were the classrooms, the after-school games, the chewing-gum and soap powder jingles, the radio announcers, the film star buccaneers, the sovereign and the flag, God and the sunburned land. Faces cajoled and winked from hoardings, newspapers announced thousands dead or maimed. Tragedies were wrapped about peas and beetroot; cast an awful blight on fish and chips.

And there were other grooves more sticky, more well-oiled that sought to bind: all those things that a little girl who knew her station ought to do. (And twenty years later a nice Adelaide lady will write that it is always the woman who comes off worst—she means me—that she has no rights by name or next-of-kinship—she means by not being married—and how can relationships survive without strong ties?—she means wedlock—and she says ladies—she means me—are denied fulfilment as women—strong word—by not having children—she means Alistair or Annabel—she says Believe me, time runs out in this respect—O lady, I believe you—and she talks of human nature being what it is, and types of situations, and free love syndromes—only she didn't spell it right. After all, she's only talking to her son.) Yet I was saved from my pliancy and submission—my ignorance, by something awkward and unyielding, prickly and resisting deep inside. I was saved by the crudity that made me pee into the bath, and revel in the tar-black shit that poured out of me and stank. Therefore I was different.

At night, alone, I pulled myself clear of the mediocrities of the world that sought to claim me. I freed my hair of its restricting pins and it shivered like a thistle bush. I stole Nan's bloomers from the drawer and escaped to the garden, their lovely silkiness all about my legs, my bare feet stung alive by stones and nettles. I crowned myself with ivy-buds and stared at the moon. I fled to a dark world that came alive only at night, nurtured by the very inattention of those others (wireless sets and electricity for them) who bound the day. I became Daphne and froze into the berry bush, Narcissus and gazed in the well. I clung to the iron of the fence and surveyed the desolation of a lane where old Mr. Stone from next but one roamed mad, where strange boys smoked tobacco in the barrel-yard, where someone shed the sanitary pad that lay bloodied and wilting further down.

My dog was my familiar in the garden; a book my companion indoors.

I approached happiness.

Yet my mother sighed at my appearance—urged me to comb my hair. My grandmother scolded for rude silence before Mrs. Dingle with gerberas and a swollen leg. And sighed too, more often than my mother; asked why I wasn't like the rest.

Mention of those fabled others became more frequent. I was urged to emulate, not Annabel from Wilderness (after all, my mother is a realist), but the more suitably plebian girl on the cover of the *Schoolgirl's Own Annual* my grandmother gave me for Christmas. I mused on her golden good looks (surely her name is Faith?—surely she wears fawn gloves?) unaware that my mother, who has forgotten how to dream, and my grandmother, who forgot so long ago she never knew, have a plan for me:

I will join the ranks of the magpie girls at the Tech School where I will learn to cook and clean and dressmake and type and book-keep and do shorthand. I will learn things like English and history and drawing incidentally. When I am fifteen I will leave school and perhaps be a commercial artist like my mother, but probably a typist. When I am seventeen I will go dancing at the Pally and I will wear a ballerina and a hooped petti and scent behind each ear. The scent will be called Junior Rose. And I will meet nice boys in white shirts and charcoal suits and shot-silk ties who smell of brilliantine and after-shave and touch me up in parked cars but always take me home. These boys will be called John or Peter or Robert (no Alistair). When I am twenty-one I will announce my engagement to one of the nice boys at a little party in the sitting-room and there will be refreshments and a silver key. I will get married in a bride's dress with a scalloped veil and go on a honeymoon to Victor—or even interstate. And then I will settle down and live in a nice house of brick with a wrought-iron gate, bought with a considerable mortgage. Soon I will be lucky because I will have lots of very nice kiddies, and will have pictures of them on a rug. Soon the very nice kiddies will be almost my age—which is twelve. I will be a housewife and shop and cook and clean and water the nice new flowers that are not really flowers but annuals or perennials with rain-water channelled neatly (no drips) through a pretty rubber hose. My husband—John or Peter or Robert—will mow the lawn. And we (I am not I any more—I am we) will have anniversaries and little parties on my birthday. And I will get pretty presents that make it all worth-while—marcasite brooches and lingerie-sets, a camera, a watch. The trees and the flowers will grow and we will not like change. The trees and the flowers will grow and we will plan for old-age. The trees and the flowers will grow and we will die. But not to worry—there will be others, always others, to take our place and live out other lives. Lives that are just as nice and proper—and mean as little, as ours.

That was the plan. That was how it invariably was.

Only this time it was different. There was a canker in the dream that was not a dream; a canker at the core— which was me.

I did not acknowledge the blight during the day when I was the one who trod the Rose Street path to school, who played under the pepper-trees and stood before the flag. I did not acknowledge it in the evening—lulled by the firelight and Tinker's snores and Reece's knitting, in the room lit with the brighter day of electric light. But when I stepped outside the enchanted circle, and entered the night of the garden, it was different.

The familiar screen which shielded me from recognition of that other world, that I saw only as a shadow picture, was gone. Cryptic messages wafted to me from all sides in all seasons: the dark green perfume of rosemary scented my fingers and clung to my skirts as I passed the hedge, the prunus-tree stuck with red paper blossoms rustled, oranges glowed through closed-in cloud; the Easter daisies fluttered, the climbing geraniums winked, lilies stared.

All about me was a wild world that broke through the symmetry of prim brick borders, neat vegetable rows, tortured roses. With the night, rats wove between the creepers on the fences that divided the yards. With winter, the galvanized iron sheds were lapped by soursobs and grass; the houses became Noah's arks, bobbing in a swollen sea.

I watched it all, and it was in the wild night garden that I discovered I did not fit into the snug electric world as others did — as they thought they did. I discovered I was different, yet I did not know where the real world lay (I was still too blinkered to know its face; I was not yet simple enough to know that it dwelt inside me, waiting to be reclaimed).

And because of this night-time half-knowledge, I tried doubly to re-enter the other circle — to be the same. I formulated long, intricate ceremonies. If I could, I would have climbed Rome's sixty-five holy steps on bended knee; as I could not, I compromised with prayers said kneeling beside my bed. I did my homework, accomplishing the hated arithmetic first; I collected the sacred images of the film star buccaneers. I submitted to home-perm afternoons and intricacies of snail-curls. I looked the same as all the other girls (shortie coat, pleated pinafore, tartan shirt like a cowboy). I conformed (gold heart on chain, autograph album, stocking-cap for Torrens, yo-yo, scooter, Malvern Star bike).

My masquerade almost succeeded.

It was spoilt by its very success.

I did not know there was a secret rule to the game I played so well (you must not believe). I did not realize that those fabled others who formulated those rules I kept too well were perplexed by my passion, confused by my too thorough conversion.

I was whole-hearted, I was extreme. I was filled with rage when I saw the missionary's daughter cheat in the exam. I was horrified when school rules were broken (not wear hats, eat in street, talk to boys). I was disgusted to find the grown-up book in the children's section (tongue kisses, skin like silk) at the library.

My rage bore witness to my weaning from the real world; gave proof of the passion locked away.

TWENTY-SIX

I HAD fits.

They were not the hot ecstasies of Puffing Billy, of the girl who fell down in the lavatory at school and was carried home in a blanket. They were colder, more contrived, and left me numb. When I sat before the fire — neat little girl in a pinafore — they dissolved to a nightmare vagueness, locked out behind the window and the night and the tapping tree. When I was carried in their icy wake, they alone were real.

I tried to explain them, excuse them, belittle them. I thought perhaps they were linked with the excitement mark on my cheek, the birthmark on my neck. I thought perhaps they were traces of some exotic degeneracy — I thought of Willie, Reece, my father's moods.

My fits threaded my life like the cord on my petticoat. They surfaced suddenly, blazed brightly — then disappeared. They illumined all my ages.

I lie in the passage. I am very small. My mother is dressed to go out (long white gloves, cartwheel hat, red and white silk spots). I cannot bear that she should go. I roll and scream on the carpet. I taste fluff and see last year's nose droppings under the table. My mother goes, but I hug my victories close. I have scratched paint from the skirting-board, made my voice hurt. I have made my mother shout; destroyed her calm perfection; tainted the beauty she wears for others.

As I grew older the fits materialized perversely when I was happy—about to taste a desire. They came when we were ready for the Odeon and Barbara Stanwyck and Robert Taylor. They came before the football match, and I was still crying when the cheers began—we got there by half-time.

It was always the same. A pure child stood aside and watched another's hate; but the one who hated watched too—saw pure child destroyed by flaming rage, self-pity's fumes (the voice goes on and on—I am bored—will it never stop?—but she can't say she's sorry—they must—she would like to be touched—but they must—hurry up and get it over, can't you?). The hate went on and on. When it was over pure child was spent and wasted, empty and weak; ready to beg forgiveness for something she never did.

As I grew older, stranger things happened.

I refused to eat; locked myself away. My grand-mother knocked in vain. Food grew colder. I longed to eat, but could not come out. When I did—red-faced, swollen-eyed—it was almost worth it. I felt calm and washed clean, emptied of all triflings of emotion. I was given (my mother said, as she always did, that I would kill her with worry) kisses and bread and butter, and the meal was still hot (warmed up in the oven).

One day I made holes in all my pants; my mother stitched with black cotton that chafed; I felt ashamed each time I walked. One day I swallowed three aspirins; pretended I had taken more (it is lovely to stare at the electric light—it hurts your eyes, makes you look sick—

I am a naughty girl — and you go quite cross-eyed); I dusted my face with Reece's powder, sucked my cheeks, said I die.

I hid in the space between the sleepout and the fence; my grandmother knew I was there, but she did not say; my mother hunted with a strap; when I came out my knees were graved with pebbles. I rubbed dirt on my legs and said I had fallen on gravel — they gave me peanuts. I was in trouble in the sitting-room — the glass swans watched — Carol came in; I hated my mother as she revealed me to my friend.

Finally, from the pages of the *True Confessions* I was not supposed to read, the films I was not supposed to watch, came inspiration.

The next time I had a fit I locked myself in the bathroom, took the razor my mother did the hairs with under her arms. I undid the top and took out the blade that quivered bluish on my hand. I sat on the edge of the bath (it is cold) and passed the blade across my wrist. I decorated myself with a pretty pattern (something like a rose) of scratches and a little blood. It did not hurt until I put it under the tap (cold, sting, sharp). But I was pleased — my wrist was rather ugly. I showed it to Nan and my mother (say next time I'll do it deeper). They looked quite worried (ha-ha); I knew I had success. My mother said How wicked; I made my grandma cry.

It is strange to sit in a classroom all neat and nice and know that the scratches are there under a cuff.

TWENTY-SEVEN

I wore a uniform. I was the same as countless others. My feet, which had gone bare all summer, were bound by socks and shoes. My body, which was a child's body still, was caged in a blouse; under the collar of the blouse snaked a tie; the tie slashed the neck of a box-pleat tunic. I wore a blazer pocketed with a gold speck that was a bird—that hovered a blue hoop—that could have been a bridge, but was a rainbow. Under the bird and the rainbow was more gold that said BUILD TOGETHER.

(And so, in February, when secateurs click and lilies die in vases, I leave the garden and the lane and summer. As my grandmother stakes chrysanthemums to wear on Mother's Day I go to another school.)

I was afraid. I waited on the verandah until I saw Joan Stott on her bicycle (I see myself: blouse, tunic, blazer, rainbow, bird). We walked to school together; went in at last year's gate. We met faces from last year too, and made a hasty raft of friendship that proved flimsy; clung together falsely in a sea of blouses and tunics and blazers and rainbows and birds.

And some of us, to show we were at ease, and that the pepper-trees and the tree with the scalloped flowers and the benches and the grey playground were still ours, dodged and hid and jumped and ran (Betty Smith falls by the lavatory, Bev King gets hit on the head). Our game stopped when a lady appeared and blew a whistle. The lady told us that we were young ladies (young ladies do not play).

We all stood still, almost as if we were frozen. (The sun is hot, my straw hat hurts my head, but I feel cold.) Even the badges and the pocket (no gloves, no stockings) and the hat did not seem to merit that. I didn't want to be a tame young lady. I was still a child. I looked at the others to see if they felt the same. They just stood still.

The lady was the headmistress. She wore ashes-of-roses, powder-blue. She had a monkey-face with round blue eyes, a chin that quivered, a mouth that let out spit. Her voice sounded full of marbles. She had golden fairy curls and crystal embroidery on dresses called ensembles; she wore lots of little buckles on her shoes. The headmistress was different from the other teachers. She had an office by the Book Room. She sat at a desk with papers and a telephone. Tea monitors took her tea on a silver tray, and there was a vase with a rose, and nursery-rhyme biscuits and a teapot that was silver. There were china ladies and a picture of a galleon; there were curtains made of lace. I knew she was a lady—she cocked her finger when she drank her tea, and pronounced lingerie in a funny way.

We went once a week to an Art Room, where a lady like a man with a protruding lip and a lumpy body drilled us in colour circles and flower-pots and horizontal borders. We went once a week to a Dressmaking Room, and I did not understand the sewing-machine; I sat at the back pretending to sew: my empty needle jumped in and out of raspberry cotton.

We went once a week to the room over the laundry, and I tried to vault a wooden box called a horse that was spiteful and reared and punched me — suddenly (in the stomach); I did the bidding of a lady who taught splits and ballet and tap down the Beach Road who had little sharp teeth. I was afraid of her and the horse and the sewing-machine and my brush going over the lines when I did the colour circle. I stood bent while a favourite (who did splits and ballet and tap) stood on my back. I got red marks and it hurt, but I was scared to say.

We went once a week to a Science Room that seemed to have a mystery. The teacher was a man. He came in the morning on a bicycle with pants caught by clips. He had a moustache; he was a foreigner. One day there were nasturtiums over the benches and all their green umbrellas and orange trumpets were cut up for our science lesson. We pulled the flowers apart and they were just petals and carpels and stamens; we put them in our books as diagrams. The room was full of sunshine that got fainter and flowers that died. (There is no mystery. The science lesson makes things shabby and commonplace. It reduces the rainbow to a name — ROY G. BIV; it sweeps away the moon — diminishes it to lunar craters. Orion, The Whale, Noah's Dove creep away — become constellations. Man is an alimentary canal.)

We did Shakespeare in English (not Shakespeare in the raw, for that would be dangerous, but Shakespeare filtered through the tales of Lamb), and there was

Peaseblossom and Mustardseed and Cobweb and Moth. I went with them to a wood near Athens; saw painted butterflies and spotted snakes and changelings and lovely boys. Wild thyme blew; I smelt oxlip, eglantine, woodbine, musk rose.

I was surprised when the lesson was over. There were no fairies in our garden (lolly papers, sickly shrubs), or in the classroom, or at Assembly where I watched the singing teacher with greasy hair feel her breast through floral nylon (and dream of a Methodist wedding in a rose garden that will never be); followed the progress of the swollen goitre beneath the senior mistress's chin.

And so we painted horizontal borders and sewed aprons and dissected nasturtiums and debated the ethics of infecting rabbits with myxomatosis. I made a beach-bag in Needlework and queen cakes in Cookery; I ran in the relay at the Sports Day and memorized 'To Autumn'. Winter came (the leaves turn yellow and flutter away); I unpicked a blue and gold band from still-new straw and stitched it to navy felt.

I was glad that winter had come (. . . and walk in a crocodile to the Railway Oval; up the Beach Road — delivery boy still on pedal, butcher treading sawdust, drapery winceyette; climb Bakewell Bridge and see trains — Brighton, Seacliff, Marino — and leave the bridge and go through a gate and no more crocodile; run — grass, willows, olives, figs — to play softball, vigaro, basketball, tennis); when it rained we couldn't do sport.

In summer it was awful (. . . get back to Rose Street

and frightened to look in the glass — so red it's really not; face like traffic lights; Catherine wheels and Roman candles; ears hurt); I rubbed at redness with ice.

Sometimes I walked up the bridge with my friend. I thought she was different from the others, but one day she had to go early (girls we watch in Grade Seven); it had happened to her as well.

(After school, when the rooms are deserted and chairs stand like trees upon the desks, when the corridors echo with cleaners' buckets and the swish of brooms, we play — and cling to the last remnants of childhood. We play as if possessed — hiding in cloakrooms, racing down aisles, peering in cupboards. I seize my friend's spectacles, and she is at my mercy — she cannot see. Her face is naked and screwed; there are circles about her eyes. She crawls up steps and stumbles between desks, knocking at chairs as she seeks. We play a strange Blindman's-buff. We whip ourselves on, whooping with terror, consumed with frenzy. I feel my friend's body as we wrestle on the floor. I force her head into the rubbish; papers and pencil shavings wreathe her hair. My heart leaps to her cries. The cleaner at the door tears us apart.)

When winter became spring (the trees are green) my friend told me she was going to be a veterinary surgeon; to be one she must go to the High School. I did not believe she would leave, but in February she was not there. When it was autumn (the green leaves turn yellow, the chrysanthemums are picked, the Easter daisies bloom) she came to see me. She looked different in the new uniform. We stood on the verandah; I tested her verbs (shorthand cannot compensate for a non-chalant: *'Voilà un livre: c'est mon livre, à moi.'*

And all my life became colourless—I did not have a friend. I grew taller and paler (Mrs. Dingle says am I ever going to stop growing); I hunched my shoulders and my head felt big. Nan said it was growing pains and took me to the doctor who asked if my period had come and gave me iron tablets. My fits got worse (I cry at night). My mother gave me Ovaltine and nerve tonic.

At school everything was changed (I am an onlooker—a spectator to other girls' friendships). I went by myself under the pepper-trees. I went up the hill by myself on Friday. I did book-keeping and shorthand and typewriting. I said could I go to the High School to my mother. She said it was too late. Anyway, what good would French be to me?

TWENTY-EIGHT

AT NIGHT I could not sleep. I listened to my mother's breathing; Tinker moved drowsily; a tap dripped. I was alone.

I thought of my aloneness and of the time when my grandmother would die. I thought of how terrible it would be to have a baby. I thought of my death. Tears ran down my cheeks; I savoured them in the dark. (It is always like this now—in the morning, when the room is full of grey, when the first birds sing, when Tinker cries to be out I will sleep. Now I lie awake.)

And as I lay between the sheets, listening to the tap and my mother's breath, feeling the weight upon my feet and the tears on my cheeks, I comforted myself.

I put my fingers between my legs. (The hand with the squashed finger plays. There are tiny hairs. Sometimes it coils them; sometimes it plucks fiercely. But always, the finger moves on. It strokes, parts, circles; a nail gathers secret pollen. The finger moves on, and the swollen cleft that was raw and ugly when I saw it in the mirror, opens: blossoms. My finger plays with a row of little lumps and hollows: is sucked into a pool.) And the agapanthus feeling sweeps deliciously; flowers and dissolves behind tight-shut eyes.

My nights became beautiful. With morning, the warmth had fled. I found hairs stuck to the sheets; my fingers smelt. And I felt guilty.

I thought of ways to defeat my hands. I stole a pair of gloves from my mother's drawer. There was a hole in one finger, but their whiteness comforted me. I wore them in bed. Sometimes I found one had come off in the morning.

I locked myself in the sleepout and took off all my clothes. I stood before the mirror—there were breasts beginning. I pushed them hard and a deep crease came between. I looked at the place that was beautiful in the night—it was uglier than ever.

I waited for what had happened to all the others to happen to me. I dreaded its coming, but wondered what it was like. One Saturday in summer I was sure it would come. My mother gave me a belt of pink elastic and a soft white pad; I put on extra pants—just in case. It was strange to see the bump showing through; strange to feel the secret between my legs, that rubbed when I sat down. (I think it must show—it doesn't; I think I must look different—I don't.) I went to see twenty cartoons with Carol, and as I ate my Eskimo Pie I brooded upon the thing I could not tell her. When I got home I went to the lavatory: it was still white. I ran out onto the lawn; I turned somersaults and waved my legs and climbed the apricot. I called out that I was not grown-up, that I was not a young lady, that I was still me— something like Peter Pan, and could do all these things. (When it does come it is a feeling of sickness; a feeling of being dirtied—I wish I was a boy.)

And hairs so fine they looked like pencilled shadows came beneath my arms. And I was ashamed of my chest and wore a cardigan all the summer.

Grown-ups were no longer fathers and mothers. They

were dirty and men and women. I stared at them in trams and saw them naked: ladies had breasts and rubber crotches; gentlemen had hair and parts like Tinker. (My mother and Nan and Reece are just as bad.)

Everything familiar became strange; I masqueraded as a child.

Every Saturday afternoon of my childhood, for as long as I could remember, I had gone to the pictures with Carol.

We queued before a lady cut off at the waist by a glass cage. We filed through a red plush foyer, down drab caramel passages, past winking EXITS and GENTS and LADIES. We gave up our tickets; entered the Moorish temple — and rococo angels strained at silent trumpets, acanthus leaves and laurel writhed, masks and pipes of Pan danced together, velvet purred, rock-crystal sang. All was as it should be (the collector shreds his tickets at the door, the lovers cuddle in the balcony, the mothers eat their dandies in the lounge, the gangs wait with their spit-bombs in the front — the manager waits for pursuit with his torch). As velvet, then silk, then gauze rippled apart, and we stood in homage to the queen and the horse, I felt the snakeskin of school slip away. There was just the darkness and the hardness of the seat; Carol's familiar odour and the dim shapes of other children staring at a screen.

(And there is Tarzan and Jane and Cheetah and Our Gang and the M.G.M. lion and Tom and Jerry. At half-time the ice-cream boys come with O.K. Peanut, Violet Crumble, Cherry Ripe, Coca-Cola, Eta Peanut,

Passionella. Carol blows balloons of American bubble-gum. The lights go out; new heroes jump into the screen.)

There had always been three ice-cream boys: various Vincenzos and Lorenzos and Nicolais, who all looked the same (shrewd eyes, oiled-satin hair, rose-bud mouth). One Saturday the most recent Vincenzo was not there — his place was taken by another. The other was beautiful, like a shy brown animal, with cinnamon eyes and nutmeg skin (I love as soon as I look). I stared hard as I bought extra peanut bars and dandies; I thought of him all the time: his face was on the flimsy in typewriting, he was there when I couldn't play my scales; there, as my fingers crept to the secret place at night.

And so, on long Sunday evenings in summer, when the streets were filled with blue, mixed with my guilt as I heard the church bells, was a strange feeling — a lovely melancholy, that was linked curiously with the ice-cream seller. The garden with its captive plants seemed to echo my longing, the cracks in the pavement smirked and urged me on. In the blue evening, when sprinklers pierced the lawns and mowers whirred and tossed fragrant spears, I walked the streets with Carol.

We walked aimlessly, without plan. Yet always, at a certain random spot — by the Queen of Angels', by the Daisy Dell, by Hook the bootmaker's, by Mrs. Newton's mulberry-tree — our footsteps faltered, as if prearranged. We stopped. And proceeded again, drawn irresistibly — by the blueness and the church bells and a web of cracks — across the Beach Road, up Fisher Terrace, to Gladstone Road.

We walked to the house that was his, and I searched

for some trace of him in fly-wire, rubbed red-brick, stained cement. We walked to the lane and stood behind the fowl-houses, the fig-trees, the compost heaps. And one day when we had brought peaches from Carol's tree, he was there — perched in the fig like Pan. We presented the fruit humbly; he took them as his due. He stared gravely. For a moment my loneliness was assuaged.

The feeling was always worse when the pictures ended and we left the rock-crystal and velvet and the sure glimpse of the ice-cream boy. It was a pale, in-between time, when our heroes dissolved behind gauze and silk and velvet, when houses seemed empty and street-lights were not yet on; when someone far away (it is always far away) plucked with one hand (it is always one hand) at a sad piano; when the roast dinner we feasted on at half past twelve had become the cold meat and pickles we had for tea.

And every Saturday evening of my childhood, after tea, for as long as I could remember, I had bought a comic with Carol.

Before the strange time began, when Tarzan and Our Gang and the M.G.M. lion were enough, I was loyal to Mandrake and Batman and the Phantom. Now, even this had changed. Unaccountably, feeling secretly ashamed, I bought the love comics that before only other girls read.

We walked to Len Roberts' Bookshop down the blue street after tea. Mothers and fathers and children had disappeared. The streets were given over to people all young, all dressed in their best, all going somewhere. There was another line now outside the Odeon; there were men in suits and ties outside the Daisy Dell. The milk-shake machines chattered, the neon lights flashed. From the Assembly Rooms we heard the wail of saxophones; were brushed by the net and sequin skirts of girls in ballerinas, and smelt their perfume, and knew it was almost time for the Prides of Erin and Military Two Steps to begin.

(The girls are beautiful, they smell of a thousand flowers. As I pay the shilling that entitles me to share the love of the pony-tailed freshman and the crew-cut instructor, the memory of their net and sequins and perfume threads the shop. It pursues us as we hurry from the lights to the nunnery of Rose Street; as we cloister ourselves behind a screen of bridesmaid's fern on Carol's verandah.)

TWENTY-NINE

I STAYED at the Technical School.

(And even as the litmus paper in the science lesson soaks up the acid and is transformed, so we soak up obediently the veiled references to our status, with which we are fed daily. Our expectations are swallowed by shorthand symbols, hammered by typewriter keys, imprisoned by the columns of a neatly-ruled ledger whose credit column never balances its debit.)

I was part of a school that was a factory, pumping forth each year, from the swollen Commercial class, the girls of fifteen who would go to work as typists and clerks. At eighteen they would be engaged, at twenty — married, at thirty — old. And these were the girls I stood with under the lacquered fig-trees in the Grade Seven photograph. (They are at their prime at the age of twelve; then, like Janet when she dreams of the spangled circus life, they can do anything. Three years later the dream will be gone, replaced by a routine that stills the small voice that asks: *Is this enough? — is this all it is?* with material objects. Not once have thoughts of the meaning of life — or its lack of meaning, which is the same — been allowed to enter their heads. They do not marvel at the lines charted on their palm, at the weeds they trample underfoot in their concrete gardens, at sun, sky, moon. All the wild poetry is locked away; only the synthetic—the secondary, is exalted.)

We are all part of a monstrous tread-wheel of compromise maintained by teachers, parents, newspapers, girls we used to know; by worthies who preside at Speech Days.

Before the Speech Day we came to school in ordinary clothes while the pleats were pressed into our tunics; while the bird was made golder, the rainbow bluer, and BUILD TOGETHER brighter below them. When they came in their ordinary clothes I saw the others transformed. Gone was the navy serge that seemed soaked in the plummy brews of menstruation, gone were the stumpy legs in socks that looked like bandages. My school-mates were transformed; they left me behind to become young ladies in nylon stockings and nail polish, who wore skirts that flapped about their calves and cummerbunds and elastic jumpers that showed their breasts.

(And all through the Technical School days it is the same: I am different. There will come a time when the other girls will all merge into one who is *they*. There will come a time when I will lock myself in the lavatory with the broken-handled brush, the stale puddles on cement, and breathe in urine to escape them; when I will keep a diary, and record in it all my loneliness and hatred, and they will find it and read it, will turn savage and hunt me. And the big-lipped art teacher will join the chase and direct it to icier wastes.

Because it must, a final day will come to free me. Yet even here they will have their victory. Then, the only girl I like, who talks constantly of Christian Witness and her Sunday School class, will betray me. She will give me the silver watch to mind that was her grandmother's — will drop it lightly into my pocket while she plays at basketball. And when she comes back to claim it, it will have gone. We will search for it everywhere — to no avail. And everyone — the big-lipped teacher, the other girls, the girl whom I admire — will think me a thief. The girl's parents will think so most of all, for they will send a lady who is a policewoman to see me.)

When it was the Speech Day the girls assumed their old disguise; all their borrowed elegance had left them. We sat together, in magpie ranks amidst the gold leaf and red plush of the Town Hall that was the picture theatre. We stood to sing 'The Nun's Chorus'. We sat, stupefied with boredom, whilst gentlemen in pepper-and-salt and ladies in simulated Persian lamb (with China weasel trimmings) paraded in turn upon the platform and pronounced cliché homilies that outdid those of the powder-blue headmistress in hypocrisy and patronage. Subtly, with silver tongues, these bland-faced directors and superintendents and inspectors reduced us to our stations; their highest modicum of praise was that one of us would make an admirable girl in an office.

Yet no director or superintendent or inspector compelled me to enter the school. I was sent there by my mother and grandmother who loved me.

My mother and grandmother were strangely innocent. Their world was narrow and circumscribed; they were lost once they strayed from their familiar paths. My mother's way was hedged with invisible briers that sheltered, as well as constricted: perplexing abstractions were made commonplace and concrete by the gold watch that ticked away the years, by the clink of coins in her purse on pay day. My grandmother's way was bound by Reece and the house and the lady across the road, by the birth and death, engagement and approaching marriage announcements in the *Advertiser*.

Because they were innocent, they were unspoiled. Once they entered the house, and the front door closed behind them, the outer world was lost—drowned in the greenness of crinkled glass. The real world sprang into being as my grandmother, my mother, Reece, and I came close. It was a delicate world that waxed and waned; constantly threatened by my grandmother's depressions and possessiveness, my mother's material-ism and secret longings, Reece's stomach that rattled, my fits. It was nurtured and protected by the roses and the grape-vines, the ivy and the lavatory-creeper that clung to the fences; by the arching berry bush, the plant that bloomed once every seven years. The real world came into being round the dining-room fire, as we toasted bread on the crooked fork; it lurked in the porcelain basin as my mother washed my hair with rain-water from the well, bloomed in the fusty bedroom as Reece soothed my head with little pats when I was sick, rose from the earth when my grandmother stooped in the garden and coaxed withered seedlings to life. In these sequestered haunts—behind the crinkled green glass and the roses, the grape-vines, the ivy and the lavatory-creeper—my grandmother's and mother's lives blossomed secretly, unacknowledged even to themselves.

This innocence had its pitfalls: they did not value

themselves; they did not realize their worth. Once they strayed from their familiar paths they were lost; their innocence tarnished. There was my grandmother's marriage that marked my mother; there was my mother's, made poetic by my father's death, by the fact of me. They did not acknowledge that they were different — that they had made me different by my upbringing in that house of the red verandah, where beauty lay all about: in Reece's ugly face, Tinker's milky gaze, my grandmother's wrinkles, the lilac shadows beneath my mother's eyes; where life, under its sham layer of studied conformity was strangely original, strangely unworldly.

Indeed, because they did not realize my difference, my mother and grandmother dreamed of the nice house with the charcoal-suited husband, where I would water the flowers with the rubber hose. They had banished the unknown; banished all uncertainty from their lives; my grandmother diminished death, by saving for her funeral. They loved me enough to wish the same for me. Surely, they reasoned, my quixotic desire to enter the High School, with its exotic Latin and French, its unknown consequences, would complicate the life they planned in all their love.

And suddenly, everything was threatened by the aridity of that world of preparatory commercialism I entered. The split that began when I ran from the sinister wooden tower, from those who claimed the Pierrot costume, to find my mother, had always been with me. I had always been two; I had always had my fits. But my two selves were complementary, they came together.

THE SCENT OF EUCALYPTUS

I was threatened. The green glass shuddered in its panes; the roses and grape-vines, the ivy and lavatory-creeper could not protect me. Even my fits eluded me; they became ceremonies I could not comprehend, as I scratched the angry patterns on my wrist. The two people I was separated. There was the pale one I despised at school; the wild one who came home — took off the shoes and the hat and the tunic, and was free.

THIRTY

Another autumn came.

Blue days were hazed with smoke from burning rubbish; green evenings washed with rain.

At dusk, the sun cast a pinkness over the garden. For a moment the autumn flowers were bright: brittle orange and red dahlias vied with mauve geraniums. The sky bent low; the garden dimmed. Wind rippled the lawn, and the dahlias and geraniums turned fickle — sprang from the earth, blazed above.

The wind rippled again; the sky garden, too, grew pale. Reds and mauves and oranges faded to indeterminate evening.

The garden was muted with acid swatches of bamboo above the fence; with darker ruffles of almond and quince, pierced by fish-shaped leaves of orange. Gum specked the apricot, stems of coral roses leapt. Only the berry bush, flecked with red, recalled the day.

Yet the dahlias and geraniums blazed on; there were rose hips everywhere. The Easter daisies trembled open; I picked them in armfuls, and the sleepout became a beehive: honey lurked at curtains, in my pillow of feathers. And I felt lazy and half asleep, yet knew that winter came.

The sun pounced on a blowfly's back and turned it green. I watered the earth, and beetles threaded the creepers with minute glistenings as they scrambled to safety. Nan knocked the leaves from the peach; carried them to burn.

Spiders were everywhere: brooding in the middle of webs, perched shameless in the air, revealing mechanical undersides. I saw five of them swinging silverly — by the apricot, the fig, between the berry bush and the clothes-line, amongst the vines.

And mists came and veiled the garden, lurked in the quince-tree at the back. The last chrysanthemums glowed, and some mauve asters, a mop of rose, a poker of larkspur. I saw the rose hips, lights along the lane. As I looked, the sky was peppered with birds.

I thought the spiders and the mists and the brightness would go on for ever.

Winter came.

I left the garden and entered the house. The kitchen was warm, suffused with smells of cooking. My grandmother's arm cradled china as she beat eggs for a cake, Reece's spit sizzled on the iron, my mother sewed on. Once more the tinsel roses shimmered in the grate, once more we sat in a tight circle about the evening — lulled by murmuring wireless, Reece's needles, the newspaper, the scratching pen.

I thought it would go on for ever.

Yet when the red-brick path is pricked with rain, when the asters are tipped with mildew, and the flower-beds sleep, all my life changes. As the chrysanthemums lurch, their petals stained with mud, my mother tells me she is to marry the man with the moustache and the R.S.L. badge who is her friend. As the last leaves fall from the trees, she tells me that we will leave the house in Rose Street. My mother and Nan and Reece and I will live with the man in a new house in a new suburb. And the chrysanthemums are sullied, the earth is hard, rain falls on iron.

Once the words were said, they radiated through the house. They resounded in the passage, hung in corners, sunk into the verandah, floated in sullen puddles on the lawn. Everything was changed. The house belonged to others. The spring that budded already in fruit-trees, the bulbs that waited in the earth, would flourish for them.

And because the garden shrank from me, I shunned it—went only to pluck a root from here, a branch from there; to dig for chrysanthemum and agapanthus, iris and rose. The old wild world was no more. The garden contracted to pot-plants on a sill: four geraniums— white and salmon, pink and rose; scraps of green that were forget-me-not and noon-flower; twigs that held promise of privet hedge and fuchsia. There was no other garden—just trees I used to climb, a clothes-line, a path that led to a lavatory.

We took down curtains and painted walls, coaxed tables from corners, found pencils and sixpences and handkerchiefs lost for years. And strangers plucked at furniture, robbed the specimen shelf, sheathed with newspaper. Charles Ebenezer came down from the wall, the harvest festival dinner-set made islands on a floor.

We lit a fire under the quince—it recalled that other fire that ushered the baker's death. Sparks wreathed the tree—there were no tart fruits, no blotting-paper stars.

THE SCENT OF EUCALYPTUS

My grandmother's skin smelt of ash. (And I will dream of quince-trees and fire twenty years later, when ice-flowers bloom at the window in a white city pelted by whiteness all night long.)

What we did not burn was thrown in the well. The fairies who stared disappeared with rusted tin and three marble nymphs that sank dully.

On the last day, when I ventured once more into the garden that was not a garden, death was all about: as a mouse — its paws drawn stiffly, its fur damp with rain; at my foot, as a one-winged blowfly stumbled; beside the plant I would not see blossom at its next seventh year; rotting leaves, abandoned snail-shells, a bone.

THE HOGARTH PRESS

This is a paperback list for today's readers – but it holds to a tradition of adventurous and original publishing set by Leonard and Virginia Woolf when they founded The Hogarth Press in 1917 and started their first paperback series in 1924.

Some of the books are light-hearted, some serious, and include Fiction, Lives and Letters, Travel, Critics, Poetry, History and Hogarth Crime and Gaslight Crime.

A list of our books already published, together with some of our forthcoming titles, follows. If you would like more information about Hogarth Press books, write to us for a catalogue:

30 Bedford Square, London WC1B 3RP

Please send a large stamped addressed envelope

Colin MacInnes
All Day Saturday

New Introduction by Tony Gould

Everybody loves Mrs Helen Bailey – everybody, that is,
except her husband Walter, who sits alone in the Australian sun, polishing his guns. For Helen, a faded *femme
fatale*, destiny seems to hold only embittered passion,
infertility and a lifetime of tea parties. But one Saturday a
young stranger arrives – and the lives and loves on the
Baileys' sheep station are altered forever.

A novel which may surprise those who know Colin
MacInnes through *Absolute Beginners*, *All Day Saturday*
is, at once, a telling portrait of a troubled marriage, a
comic evocation of life in the Bush, and a classical drama
– where the fates of many are decreed in a day.

Graham McInnes
The Road to Gundagai

New Introduction by Robertson Davies

Lauded by John Betjeman, birthplace of Germaine Greer, home of Dame Edna Everage and source of Foster's lager, the city of Melbourne is regarded as one of the most gracious in the world. But not by the novelist Angela Thirkell – uprooted from England in 1919 with her two sons, Graham and Colin McInnes – who viewed all Australians as being both down and under. The boys, however, took to Australia with gusto, and this is the memoir, wonderfully, wittily told, of their adventures in that strange, compelling land. *The Road to Gundagai* shows us 'boyhood in essence' (Angus Wilson), but it is, too, a portrait of a beautiful city, an astonishing country, a devastating mother – 'a work of literary art' (*Times Literary Supplement*).

David Garnett

Lady into Fox &
A Man in the Zoo

New Introduction by Neil Jordan

'The most amazingly good story . . . I think it is
perfectly done'

So wrote H.G. Wells when he reviewed *Lady into Fox* in
1922. This parable about a young Edwardian woman
who turns into a fox before her astonished husband's eyes
is published here with the equally delightful novella
which David Garnett wrote two years later about the first
man to be exhibited at London Zoo. Beautifully illus-
trated with Ray Garnett's original wood-engravings,
these are piquant love stories combined with exquisite
observations of our social behaviour. They have too
the timeless quality of the fable, revealing not only the
idiosyncrasies of the animal kingdom, but also the
vagaries of the human heart.

David Garnett

Aspects of Love

A young boy, a beautiful actress, an elderly aristocrat – troubled desire and tangled emotions flowering against the glowing backgrounds of Southern France, Italy and Paris. Such are the 'aspects of love' in this compelling, passionate novel, the source of Andrew Lloyd Webber's celebrated musical.

J.L. Carr
A Day in Summer

New Introduction by D.J. Taylor

This, J. L. Carr's first novel, displays the same rare gifts as later works such as *The Harpole Report* and the Booker-shortlisted *A Month in the Country* and *The Battle of Pollocks Crossing*.

It is a festive summer's day when Peplow, a quiet bank clerk, arrives in Great Minden to shoot the killer of his son. But his task is complicated when he meets a couple of old wartime colleagues – only two of the townsfolk with problems of their own. Written with a wry under-standing of the tragedy and folly of everyday lives, this is a blackly comic thriller, moving towards an ominous climax – for little can the folk of Great Minden suspect how their day will end.

Neil Jordan
Night in Tunisia

Introduced by Sean O'Faolain

'One of the most memorable pieces of fiction to be published in recent years' – *Time Out*

The title story of Neil Jordan's stunning collection was described by Sean O'Faolain as 'one of the most remarkable stories that I have read in Irish storytelling since, or indeed before, Joyce'. Neil Jordan's powerful, distinctive voice has established him as one of the most important and original of contemporary writers. *Night in Tunisia* was awarded the *Guardian* Fiction Prize.